THE BIGGEST LOSER

YOUR PERSONAL PROGRAMME FOR PERMANENT WEIGHT LOSS

WITH
ANGIE DOWDS &
RICHARD CALLENDER

An Hachette UK Company
www.hachette.co.uk

First published in Great Britain in 2011 by Hamlyn,
a division of Octopus Publishing Group Ltd
Endeavour House
189 Shaftesbury Avenue
London WC2H 8JY
www.octopusbooks.co.uk

ISBN 978-0-600-62271-0

A CIP catalogue record for this book is available from
the British Library.

Colour reproduction in the UK.
Printed and bound in Spain.

10 9 8 7 6 5 4 3 2 1

All reasonable care has been taken in the preparation
of this book, but the information it contains is not
meant to take the place of medical care under the
direct supervision of a doctor. Before making any
changes in your health and fitness regime, always con-
sult a doctor. Any application of the ideas and information contained in this book is at the reader's sole
discretion and risk. Neither the author nor the publisher
will be responsible for any injury, loss, damages, actions,
proceedings, claims, demands, expenses and costs
(including legal costs or expenses) incurred in any way
arising out of following the exercises in this book.

'The Biggest Loser' is produced by Shine Limited for
ITV1 based on the format owned by Reveille LLC.

'The Biggest Loser' is a registered trademark of Shine
Limited. All rights reserved.

General Editor Gill Paul
Trainers Richard Callender and Angie Dowds
Dietician Laura Clark BSc RD

Publishing Director Stephanie Jackson
Senior Editor Leanne Bryan
Copy Editor Katie Hardwicke
Proofreader Corrine Ochiltree
Indexer Dorothy Frame

Deputy Art Director Yasia Williams-Leedham
Design and Art Direction Nicky Collings
Photographer John Davis
Photographer's Assistant Dave Foster
Make-up Artist Victoria Barnes
Home Economist Lizzie Harris
Home Economist's Assistant Katy Greenwood
Picture Research Manager Giulia Hetherington
Production Manager Peter Hunt

Shine would like to thank:
Wayne Davison, John Gilbert, Jessica Hannan,
Fiona McDonald, Jamie Munro, Claire Nosworthy,
Lisa Perrin, Paolo Proto, Karen Smith, and Gordon
Wise of Curtis Brown.

Jordan Fitness, in the industry for over 20 years,
specialize in the design, manufacture and supply
of commercial quality functional fitness equipment.
Jordan is proud to have supplied the fitness
equipment used in this Biggest Loser UK book.

PHOTOGRAPHIC CREDITS All photographs are by
John Davis with the exception of the following:

Alamy Chris Rout 184; Maskot Bildbyrå AB 187; Tetra
Images 10; Tim Hill 3.

Fotolia Andres Rodriguez 91; info2me 175; John
Goldstein 32; Ljupco Smokovski 17; Okea 192
below right.

Contents

On your marks!

You're here. You've bought the book. You've made the decision to become a Biggest Loser. And we all know why.

Maybe you've been finding for some time now that being overweight isn't much fun. You'd like to have more energy but those kilos are dragging you down. You'd like to be able to wear clothes with a shape to them, rather than tents. Maybe you've got a big date coming up – a wedding or a school reunion. Perhaps you've recently seen a candid photograph that sent shivers down your spine. You've been thinking you should get round to losing weight for some time. Well, the time is now.

Becoming a Biggest Loser
The Biggest Loser team is used to dealing with people with serious weight problems – from those who've been given a wake-up call by their doctor to those who want to drop a few dress sizes and revisit the thinner person they used to be. We've seen it all, we've heard all the excuses, and when it comes to losing weight, we know what works, whether you've got 2 kilos or 20 kilos to lose. There are no new-fangled ideas here, simply a tried-and-tested, infallible method of weight loss that involves eating less and doing lots of fat-burning exercise – but with a twist. We're going to engage you not just on a practical level, but also emotionally, so you can work out why you're eating too much and how to change that long term.

For your part, you've got to commit right now – and stay committed. You won't be able to eat as much as you're used to but you won't go hungry either, because starvation doesn't bring about permanent weight loss. The exercise programme is an integral part of the Biggest Loser plan, not something you can take or leave. You'll have to change your daily routine to fit exercise sessions into your week if you want to be a successful Loser.

But trust us. This is a programme that not only works for the folks you've seen being transformed at the Biggest Loser house on telly, but for real people, too. It works because we use a very simple equation: burn more calories than you eat. And then keep on burning. The simple combination of a good, balanced diet and serious exercise is a winning one!

Heads up!
You won't have to tot up calories on the Biggest Loser plan, avoid whole food groups or exist on diet milkshakes. We've created a tasty six-week healthy eating plan and a tough six-week fitness plan that will make you lose weight steadily.

Follow the programme properly, really throw yourself into it, and you'll lose the weight you want to lose, but at a rate that will be sustainable. You won't put it back on again, because you'll have lost it sensibly, developed new eating and exercise habits, and you'll be feeling so much better by the end of the six weeks that you won't ever want to look back.

Just like the contestants in the Biggest Loser house, if you follow our methods you'll see the results – fast.

INTRODUCTION

Before **Miriam** After

Feeling fantastic

That's what it's all about, isn't it? We all want to live longer, and the Biggest Loser plan will get you to the place where your odds of living a long life are much higher than they were before. Maybe you've had a health scare and that's why you want to sort yourself out. Perhaps you're looking older than your years. Maybe you feel embarrassed about the way you look in a swimsuit or you simply feel fat. All of these are important reasons to lose weight. Wanting to look attractive is just as valid as heart health if that is what matters to you.

In the programme, you'll set yourself a short- and then some long-term goals – maybe 6 kg (roughly a stone) in 6 weeks, then 32 kg (5 stone) in a year. It could be more. Once you've mastered the first 10 kg (1.6 stone), the second, and maybe even the third, will go as well. We'll guide you through the process.

Setting goals works! They give you something to aim for in the short-term, and each time you hit your target you'll get a huge boost that will spur you on to your next success.

Hit the scales

There's plenty of research to suggest that about half of us underestimate our weight by 25 per cent – and we bet you're in that half. Before you start the programme you're going to have to stand on the scales and be honest with yourself. Shock is good. It prepares you for change. Set your goal while that figure is fresh in your mind. Use the chart on page 15 to help you aim for a weight that is healthy for your height and build. We'll also give you lots of tips on how to keep focused on that goal, from keeping a food diary, taking photos to chart your changing appearance and plenty of recipes to keep hunger at bay and introduce fresh, healthy and tasty food to sustain you on your journey to the new, thinner you.

Now start!

We're going to sort you out, from top to bottom, with a weight-loss programme that works. There will be difficult days. You might get frustrated when the numbers on your scales don't drop as fast as you'd like; you'll feel irritated that you have to head out into the rain to exercise on a wintry Monday morning; you'll feel annoyed that the office cream cakes are no longer on the cards. But wait! Something else will be happening at the same time. You'll get compliments about how well you look. Your trousers will be a little looser at the waist. Your dress will drape instead of cling. Your face will look leaner, trimmer and younger. Your feet will fit in your shoes. You are losing weight. And you are feeling good.

You can do this because you want change – you know you do – and the Biggest Loser programme can offer you a way of achieving it. If you follow this programme, you will lose weight, you will get fitter and healthier, and you will look and feel a whole lot better. That's a promise!

JANUAR

SUNDAY	MONDAY	TUE
	New Year's Day	
	1	
		8

Start
Diet
Today!

Setting your goals

You might be raring to start the Biggest Loser weight-loss programme straight away, but take time first of all to set realistic goals and plan strategies that will ensure it fits in with your lifestyle. Get ready to be slim and healthy, because this is the programme that is going to succeed where all others have failed!

Are you ready?

The Biggest Loser weight-loss programme is simple, but that doesn't mean it's an easy ride. Be prepared to work hard and always keep the reasons why you want to lose weight firmly in your mind. Over the following pages we'll show you how to get organized, so that you can begin to make a change.

Before you begin, it's sensible to keep your expectations in perspective – even the hardest work won't produce a miracle overnight, and if you have a lot of weight to lose you need to be prepared for this to take a little time. Healthy weight loss is never instant. Keeping healthy – and keeping the weight off – is a steady process with long-lasting results. Take each week at a time, celebrating the weight that you lose, and this will spur you on to your next goal. Full commitment will get maximum rewards. Be realistic about your goals, the way you'll look when you meet them, and the time it's going to take to get there, and you'll find the journey that much easier. The good news is that this programme works and keeps on working for years and years to come.

Visualize the new you

Try to imagine what you'll look like when you lose weight – if you've got an image of Cheryl Cole or Robert Pattinson in mind, use that to motivate you but keep your expectations real – many celebrities have the help of make-up artists and airbrushing to achieve their perfect looks. To get a clearer guide to the new you, look at photos of yourself before you put on the weight.

Getting underway

Tomorrow is definitely another day, but it's also a great excuse for putting off change indefinitely. 'I'll start tomorrow' won't get you thin – there's always another tomorrow. Set a firm date for beginning your weight-loss journey and stick to it.

Don't plan to start too far ahead: a few days' time will keep up the momentum of your decision. Write the date on your calendar, put a note on the fridge and set an alert on your mobile. The more you remind yourself, the more likely it is that you'll actually begin.

You need to get yourself organized, practically and emotionally. Stock up with healthy food, purchase anything you need to get your fitness plan off to a flying start, join a gym if you plan to get fit in a professional environment, and get yourself into the right mind-set to succeed. Here's how…

Create a support network
Tell your most supportive friends and family members about your plans. Make sure they know how important it is to you and are prepared to back you to the hilt. Avoid the friends who say you look 'fine' just the way you are or egg you on to have that second biscuit. Choose the ones who will help to keep you propped up and motivated throughout the

Before **Carol** After · Before **Mark** After

process, and who will compliment you as the trim, fit person inside begins to emerge. It will be harder to cheat or give up, if you've got your own team of cheerleaders behind you.

Choose a date a couple of days from now and decide that you will begin on this day – no matter what life throws at you in the meantime.

Buy a weight-loss notebook

You'll use your Biggest Loser notebook to chart your progress. In it you will analyze your emotional responses to food (see page 22) and the reasons why you want to lose weight (see page 18), as well as noting what you actually eat and drink, and you'll chart your rapidly decreasing weight. Keep this notebook with you throughout the programme.

Take some 'before' photos

It's a good motivational trick to strip down to your underwear before you begin and take a few photos. Tape one to the inside of the fridge and another in your Biggest Loser notebook. Look at these pictures often: they'll remind you why you want to lose weight. Get used to looking at yourself naked over the weeks to come – you'll see fat disappearing and the jiggly bits toning up. When you glance back at the 'before' photos, you'll see just how much you've achieved.

| Before | **Michaela** | After | | Before | **Jamie** | After |

Determining your weight-loss goals

If you have a lot of weight to lose, don't expect to shed it all during the six weeks of the Biggest Loser programme. Slow and steady will gain the biggest rewards.

Unless you have 24-hour support and monitoring by experts, rapid weight loss can be unhealthy and counterproductive. Most people who lose weight quickly put it all back on again before too long – and more (see page 16).

It is realistic to aim to lose between 0.5 and 1 kg (about 1 to 2 lb) a week. So, over the six weeks of the programme you can expect to lose between 3 and 6 kg (6 to 12 lb). In fact, if you follow the exercise programme religiously, you'll probably lose more than this. It may well be only a small percentage of the total weight you want to lose, but set this target now and then set a new one in six weeks' time. Some people lose weight more quickly than others, but everyone who follows this programme will lose weight.

If you want to lose 63 kg (10 stone) altogether, it might feel overwhelming, but by breaking your overall goal down into a series of achievable mini-targets, you'll stay motivated more easily.

The contestants in the Biggest Loser TV series lose weight at a faster rate than is advised in this book, but you must remember that they are under constant medical supervision – and you will not be.

Noting your weight

Before you start the programme you need to step on the scales and take your 'before' weight. Weigh yourself first thing in the morning, without clothes, after going to the loo, and jot down your weight in your notebook. If your scales also give body fat percentage, note this as well. Throughout the programme you will weigh yourself once a week, and it should always be first thing in the morning. This weekly check will soon begin to show you how well you're progressing.

What's your BMI score?

Obesity is calculated using a formula called body mass index (BMI), which divides a person's weight in kilograms by their height in metres squared. You don't have to do the maths yourself – take a look at the chart opposite to work out where you fall. A BMI of between 18.5 and 24 is considered healthy, 25–29 overweight, 30–40 obese, and over 40 severely obese. You'll need to determine your correct height and weight before you calculate your BMI.

How much do you need to shift?

BMI is usually a good indication of whether you are at a healthy or unhealthy weight for your height, but if you are very muscular you could find yourself in the overweight bracket even if you are trim and fighting fit. However, if you are heading into the 30+ category, it is more than likely your weight is putting your health at risk. Look across the table to see the weight you would have to be to achieve a BMI of 25 or less. Ideally, your final target weight should be one that puts you firmly into the healthy BMI category but if this is too big a goal, why not start by trying to lose 10 per cent of your current weight? This will still have a major pay-off for your health.

BMI chart

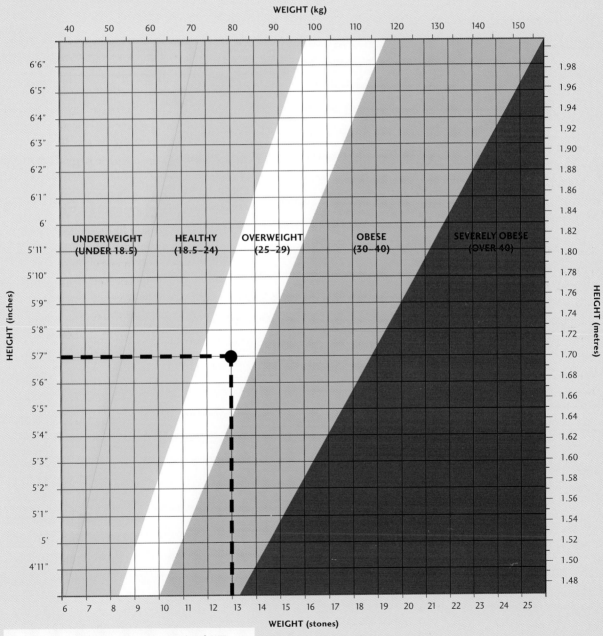

WEIGHT (kg)

UNDERWEIGHT
(UNDER 18.5)

HEALTHY
(18.5–24)

OVERWEIGHT
(25–29)

OBESE
(30–40)

SEVERELY OBESE
(OVER 40)

HEIGHT (inches)

HEIGHT (metres)

WEIGHT (stones)

In the example given, a person with a height of 5'7"
and weighing 13 stone can be seen to be overweight.

Taking things slowly

To achieve a healthy weight loss of between 0.5 and 1 kg (about 1 to 2 lb) a week, you need to create a 'calorie shortfall' by using between 500 and 1,000 more calories per day than you consume. The best way to achieve this is by eating less and exercising more.

Losing between 0.5 and 1 kg (1 to 2 lb) every week is sustainable because you'll be dropping the weight at a healthy rate and you shouldn't be starving. Most dieters fail because they are hungry and miserable. If you are eating enough to stay energetic, comfortable and happy, your chances of success are much higher.

Crash diets don't work

It should be that the less you eat and the more you exercise, the more weight you will lose; however, sudden, extreme weight loss is dangerous for your health, putting every organ in your body under pressure. Our bodies are finely tuned instruments and if they don't get the calories they need to sustain body functions, they switch into famine mode. Down goes your metabolic rate, which is responsible for burning calories and fat. Research shows that very low-calorie diets can make your metabolic rate drop by up to 45 per cent.

If you start to eat normally again after a crash diet, your body will remember that it was recently starving and will tend to store calories so that it is well prepared for any future famine – and the pounds will return with a vengeance!

If you manage a calorie shortfall of 3,500 a week, you should lose 0.5 kg (1 lb).

A new way of living

What does work is taking things slowly, changing your old, unhealthy habits for new ones that will see you eating well, exercising regularly and making healthy lifestyle choices. It can take time to banish the old habits, but with a little practice your new lifestyle will soon become the norm and you won't be tempted by junk food or hours spent slumped in front of the telly. You'll want to continue, because you'll feel fantastic – lighter, more energetic and healthier – and that is the key to long-term success.

What does your doctor say?

Being overweight has a very real impact on your health. Women with a waist measurement of more than 80 cm (32 in) and men over 94 cm (37 in), have an increased risk of heart attack or stroke. Before you embark on any exercise programme and make massive changes to your diet, it's worth seeing your doctor for a check-up, especially if you have a pre-existing health condition or have not exercised for some time.

The power of positive thinking

For your programme to be successful, you have to believe it will be. You have to remind yourself every single day of why you are losing weight and becoming fit, and the best way to do that is to set out your reasons at the start.

In your Biggest Loser notebook, write down five reasons why you want to make changes. Do you want to feel gorgeous on your wedding day? Have enough energy to run around the park playing football with your kids? Wear a bikini on your next beach holiday? Feel more sexy? Look the part for the job you want? Be the Biggest Winner? What is really motivating you to shift the kilos and get fit? What matters most?

Now think about how you are going to look and feel in six weeks' time – and how you'll feel when you reach your final target weight. Write this down. Think about all the ways in which your life is going to be different and better. At the bottom of the list write: 'I will succeed!' Because you will!

Mind games

No matter how positive you feel at the outset, your old doubts and low self-esteem may creep back in at some stage. You may even consider throwing in the towel, but send those negative thoughts straight back. Say firmly to yourself, as often as you can: 'I am a successful Biggest Loser', 'I am losing weight and getting fit', 'I love my new life'. Keeping these thoughts at the front of your mind will not only trick your brain into believing what it's told, but it will also keep the negative and unhelpful thoughts at bay.

There's nothing like a compliment to boost your self-esteem, and you'll be getting plenty of them as all your hard work begins to show.

Don't give up...

- If you slip up and eat three chocolate bars in a row, don't panic. Lapses are perfectly normal and are part of the process of change.
- Do some extra cardio exercises (see page 92) and get straight back on the programme.
- Don't let others lead you astray. You may find that some of your friends and family feel threatened by your resolve – and your success – and will try to tempt you to resume your old habits. Understand that this is their problem. You've got yourself sorted.
- Expect to feel low and frustrated some of the time. You will be tired and your muscles may be screaming! Think of this as productive pain and use it as fuel to push you forwards.
- Take it one day and one kilo at a time. Set realistic short-term goals and when you reach them, don't just celebrate – set a new one! Accept compliments and believe them. You will be looking better every single day!

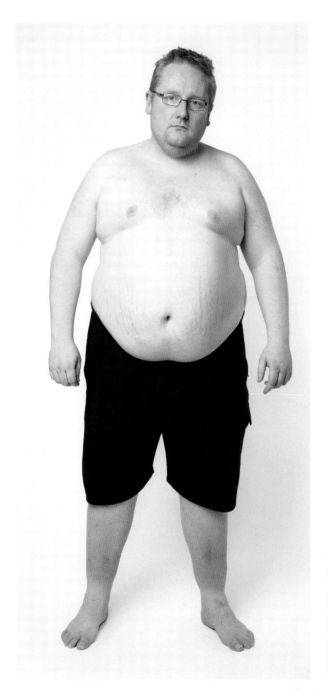

Before   **Kevin**   After

Your healthy eating programme

The Biggest Loser weight-loss programme offers lots of healthy-eating choices to suit all tastes. Once you start to follow it, you can expect to feel – and see – the changes within a week. And that's a promise.

Eat well, live well

To some people, the words 'healthy eating' may conjure up images of bland tofu and plates of unappealing green leaves. The truth is that healthy eating is anything but boring. In the healthy eating programme, we've come up with some fantastic recipes that you'll enjoy cooking. You'll have plenty of variety and – most importantly – plenty to eat!

Unlike many diets, you won't have to sit with a calculator totting up the calories in every last morsel that passes your lips. However, it's important to become 'calorie aware' – knowing which foodstuffs have a high calorie count and which are low in calories. By maintaining a calorie shortfall in your diet, you'll lose weight steadily. Simply following the recipes and menu plans in the programme will help to ensure that you meet that shortfall.

The Biggest Loser healthy eating programme is based on fresh, home-cooked foods, because by cooking meals from scratch you know exactly what ingredients are going into them and there are no high-calorie surprises. You can also ensure that you get the nutrients your body needs by choosing a certain number of portions from each food group per day (see page 33).

A balanced diet will not only encourage healthy, sustainable weight loss, but will also help to slow down the degenerative signs of ageing, reduce your risk of diabetes, heart disease and immune problems, lift your mood, banish niggling health problems, encourage healthy sleep patterns, improve your skin and hair, and, best of all, provide the basis for delicious, nutritious meals that keep you full and fighting fit – ready for all that exercise you're going to be doing!

Changing your diet

Working out what you are eating, when and why is a useful exercise before you start the programme, because understanding why you overeat will help you to avoid the triggers or handle them differently.

If you are overweight, you have probably been overeating and, very likely, eating too many of the wrong foods. It's fine to have a takeaway every now and then, but if they are the mainstay of your diet, along with a litre of cola and a packet of chocolate digestives, you'll need to make some changes. Convenience food is often the easy option for a busy lifestyle but by adapting to cooking for yourself with fresh ingredients, you will be taking a major step in the right direction to losing weight.

When you eat, and how often, can also be key to weight gain – and weight loss. Keeping to regular mealtimes and avoiding snacking is a simple rule that reaps huge rewards.

What's also very likely is that you are overeating for a reason. Maybe you are sad or lonely, or even just bored. Can you absent-mindedly eat three bags of crisps while you watch telly? Do you reach for a box of chocolates when you've had an argument with your partner? Has your self-esteem hit rock bottom, so you think: 'I just don't care'? A food diary can help you to recognize these negative associations.

Keeping a food diary

Use your notebook to jot down everything you eat and drink for the next week – and that means everything. Make a note of the time and exactly what passed your lips, then write down how you were feeling. For example, you ate the doughnut with your morning latte because your colleague was having one and you felt pressurized; you drank the bottle of wine and ate a packet of cashews because you were feeling lonely. Write it down immediately after eating rather than trying to remember everything at the end of the day. You'll probably be surprised by how much you eat, but perhaps even more surprised that there is a pattern to your eating, and that your mood and your activities definitely play a role in your food choices.

You'll keep your food diary going throughout the programme, too, because keeping tabs on your daily diet will help you to stay in control.

Calories in vs calories out

The biggest change to your diet will be the number of calories you consume. The healthy diet that forms part of the programme is balanced, nutritious and low in foods that are high in calories. The programme has been designed to ensure that you achieve that all-important calorie shortfall that will lead to steady weight loss. We've done the maths for you and all you have to do is follow it. If you are substituting your own recipes, though, or including favourite foods, be sure to note the portions or check the calorie counts either on the packaging, or by using a calorie counting book or website.

Top tips for sustainable weight loss

Weight loss is simple when you bear in mind the factors that can make you a dieting winner – or, ideally, Biggest Loser. If you are ready to succeed, read o

EAT REGULAR MEALS
Don't go for more than three or four hours without food. This regulates your metabolism and helps you to tell the difference between real physical hunger and cravings that have an emotional basis.

3

EAT BALANCED MEALS
A range of fruit and vegetables should provide the bulk of your diet, because they fill you up, contain lots of vital nutrients and are almost always low in calories. But it's important to eat proteins and carbohydrates to complete the balance and ensure your body gets all the vitamins and minerals it needs.

2

KEEP A FOOD DIARY
Jotting down everything that passes your lips throughout the day will help you to keep tabs on your overall intake and you'll get to know your food habits and what influences them. It's all too easy to overlook that handful of peanuts or the biscuit with your coffee – particularly if you are a grazer.

4

NEVER SKIP BREAKFAST
Breakfast helps to kickstart your metabolism and stops you turning to high-calorie snacks for energy later in the day.

5 GO LOW-FAT

Whenever there are alternatives, choose the low-fat versions of the foods you want to eat. Make simple changes to the way you cook: using nonstick pans or oil spray rather than butter or oil; steaming and grilling rather than frying; choosing low-fat yogurt instead of cream, and cutting off all visible fat from meat.

6 GET ACTIVE

This couldn't be simpler. Exercise – even running up the stairs at work or walking briskly to the shops – burns calories. The more you exercise, the more calories you'll burn and the more weight you'll lose.

7 PLAN AHEAD

Dump the junk in your cupboards and fill your fridge with healthy, nutritious foods. If the foods that made you fat are still in the house, you'll be tempted to eat them. Plan your meals and snacks well in advance and head out for the weekly shop with a list of what you need to buy. Don't shop when you're hungry – it's always disastrous.

DON'T DENY YOURSELF

Trying to avoid foods you enjoy is likely to make you crave them and that's when you could be tempted to binge. The Biggest Loser programme gives you a daily calorie allowance for 'treats' so you can indulge yourself – just a little. You'll need willpower if these are the foods you associate with overeating but that's all part of winning the battle.

A balanced diet

A balanced diet is composed of five food groups: fruit and vegetables; carbohydrates; protein; dairy; and foods high in fat and sugar. These contain all the nutrients your body needs to function to the max. Making sure your plate includes all these groups in the right proportions is a simple way to get all you need from your meal to nourish your body, keep healthy and lose weight.

Fruit and vegetables
These should cover half your plate. Whether you choose salad, sliced fruit or a variety of different vegetables, you'll be adding crucial vitamins and minerals to your diet as well as fibre. And eating as many different fruits and vegetables as you can will ensure that you are getting a wide variety of nutrients that can boost overall health and wellbeing.

Protein
This should cover a quarter of your plate. Opt for healthy sources of protein, such as lean meats, fish (aim for oily ones, such as salmon and mackerel twice a week), chicken and other poultry, eggs, pulses, dairy produce, nuts, seeds and tofu. Protein is very important for maintaining the body's vital functions and for muscle development, which in turn boosts your metabolism, so getting enough

is crucial. Try to avoid fatty sources of protein, such as processed and heavily marbled meats.

Carbohydrates
These should cover the last quarter of your plate. Carbohydrates are needed to supply the body with fuel. The less 'white' they are, the better. Whole foods, such as wholemeal bread and brown rice, are best because they contain the most fibre and are packed full of essential vitamins. What's more, they keep you feeling fuller for longer, as they take longer to digest.

Avoid the 'no-carb' dieting trap
Carbohydrates are an important source of energy, and they fuel your brain and muscles. Their bad name tends to come from the fact that we overeat them and pair them with more fattening foods, such as butter with our bread, cheese on jacket potatoes and creamy sauces with pasta.

What about fat?
You should include a small amount of fat in your diet as it is essential for the maintainance of body function. However, fat is high in calories and its consumption should be limited to encourage weight loss. That's why this programme suggests that you use low-fat products whenever possible. Go for healthy fats, such as vegetable or olive oil, and low-fat dairy produce. Eat nuts and seeds in moderation.

Fruit and vegetables

50%
(for example apples, blueberries, apricots, tomatoes, carrots, aubergines, broccoli, courgettes, peppers, butternut squash, spinach)

Protein
25%
(for example lean meat, poultry, eggs, pulses, dairy, nuts, seeds, tofu)

Carbohydrates
25%
(for example wholemeal bread and pasta, brown rice, grains)

Portion sizes

You can still put on weight while eating healthy food if you eat too much of it. That's why the Biggest Loser weight-loss programme recommends that you watch your portion sizes.

It's easier to count the number of portions of each food group that you eat in a day than to tot up all the calories, so you will be given a daily allowance of a certain number of portions of each group (see page 33) – but make sure you stick to the portion sizes listed here.

Fruit and vegetables

Men can eat eight portions of fruits, vegetables or salad per day; women can eat five. A portion is:

- 3 heaped teaspoons of raw, cooked, frozen or canned vegetables (or 80 g/3¼ oz)
- 1 side salad the size of a cereal bowl
- A handful of olives (in brine)
- 1 medium tomato or 7 cherry tomatoes
- 2 small fruits, for example plums, apricots, satsumas
- 1 medium fruit, for example apple, orange, pear, small banana
- 1 slice of very large fruit the size of your hand, for example melon, pineapple
- ½ grapefruit
- 1 cup of berries, for example a dozen grapes or 7 strawberries
- 3 heaped tablespoons of cooked fruit

- 1 heaped tablespoon or small handful of dried fruit, for example raisins or 3 dried apricots
- 3 tablespoons of canned fruit in natural juice
- 1 small glass (150 ml/¼ pint) unsweetened fruit juice (limit to one glass daily)

Protein

Men can eat three portions of protein per day; women can eat two. A portion is:

- 70–90 g (2½–3½ oz) cooked lean beef, pork, lamb, ham, turkey, chicken or oily fish (for example salmon or trout)
- 150 g (5 oz) grilled, poached or steamed white fish or seafood
- 1 can (130 g/4¼ oz drained) tuna in brine or spring water
- 1 can (120 g/3¾ oz) sardines or mackerel in tomato sauce or brine
- 3 fish fingers (grilled)
- 2 eggs
- 5 tablespoons (200 g/7 oz) baked beans
- 4 tablespoons (150 g/5 oz) cooked lentils
- 5 tablespoons (200 g/7 oz) cooked beans or peas, for example red kidney beans, butter beans, chickpeas
- 125 g/4 oz soya beans, tofu or Quorn
- 2 tablespoons pine nuts
- 2 tablespoons (75 g/3 oz) reduced-fat hummus
- 1 tablespoon (25 g/1 oz) unsalted nuts
- 2 heaped tablespoons seeds, for example sunflower or pumpkin

Carbohydrates

On the programme, men can eat eight portions of carbohydrates per day; women can eat six. A portion is:

- 3 tablespoons (35 g/1½ oz or small bowl) breakfast cereal
- 2 tablespoons (25 g/1 oz) unsweetened, untoasted muesli
- 2 tablespoons (25 g/1 oz) dry porridge oats
- 1 slice medium thickness (35 g/1½ oz) bread or toast
- ½ bread roll or ½ bagel
- ½ pitta or 1 mini pitta bread
- 1 small plain chapatti
- ½ small naan bread
- 3 crispbreads
- 3 small crackers
- 2 egg-sized (100 g/3¾ oz) potatoes
- ½ a medium baked potato or sweet potato (about the size of a computer mouse)
- 2 tablespoons mashed potato (without added fat)
- 2–3 heaped tablespoons (50 g/2 oz) cooked pasta, noodles, couscous, or bulgar wheat (25 g/1 oz uncooked)
- 1–2 heaped tablespoons (50 g/2 oz) cooked rice (25 g/1 oz uncooked)
- 1 small (125 g/4 oz) plantain
- 1 slice (75 g/3 oz) yam
- 2 small oatcakes
- 1 plain digestive biscuit
- 1 crumpet or 1 scotch pancake
- ½ English muffin
- ½ plain or fruit scone

Fats and sugars

Men can have five portions of fats and sugars per day; women can eat three. A portion is:

- 1 level teaspoon (5 g) margarine
- 1 level teaspoon (5 g) monounsaturated or polyunsaturated oil, for example olive oil, rapeseed oil, soya oil or sunflower oil
- 2 level teaspoons (10 g) low-fat spread
- 1 level teaspoon (5 g) tahini
- 1 level teaspoon (5 g) butter, coconut cream, ghee or mayonnaise
- 2 level teaspoons (10 g) low-fat (light or extra light) mayonnaise
- 2 level teaspoons (10 g) salad cream
- 4 level teaspoons (20 g) low-fat salad cream
- 2 level teaspoons (10 ml) single or soured cream or half-fat crème fraîche
- 2 level teaspoons (10 ml) low-fat French dressing
- 50 ml (2 fl oz) reduced-fat coconut milk
- 1 teaspoon (5 g) sugar, jam or honey

Snacks

Women have an allowance of 100 calories a day for snacks and men have 200. A snack is approximately:

- 60g (2¼ oz) low-fat cheese
- Fresh fruit slices equal to 80g (3¼ oz)
- 2 oatcakes, rice cakes or crispbreads with low-fat cream cheese or yeast extract
- 1 low-fat yogurt
- 1 fat-free frozen yogurt
- 1 treat-sized chocolate bar
- A handful of nuts or seeds

- **A handful of dried fruit**
- **1 crumpet with low-fat spread**
- **2 jaffa cakes**
- **1 small bowl of air-popped plain popcorn**
- **1 pot of no-added-sugar jelly**
- **1 pot of low-fat chocolate mousse**
- **1 pot of low-fat crème caramel**
- **2 squares of dark chocolate**
- **2 tablespoons hummus with vegetable batons**
- **2 tablespoons low-fat dip with vegetable batons**

What about dairy?

Dairy doesn't have its own section of your dinner plate because it falls into the protein category and is a valuable source of this vital nutrient. It can be used in cooking, drinks, snacks or to enhance the flavour of foods, but low-fat options should be opted for whenever possible. Three portions a day for both men and women also ensures that you're getting all the calcium that your body needs. A portion is:

- **250 ml (8 fl oz) skimmed milk**
- **200 ml (7 fl oz) semi-skimmed milk or soya milk**
- **1 small pot (150 g/5oz) low-fat yogurt, fromage frais or soya dessert**
- **200 g (7 oz) low-fat yogurt**
- **1 pot (150 g/5 oz) cottage cheese**
- **25 g (1 oz) – the size of a matchbox – medium-fat cheese, for example Edam, Camembert, Cheddar or other hard cheeses**
- **50 g (2 oz) low-fat soft cheese, for example light cream cheese**

Following the healthy eating plan

The average woman needs about 2,000 calories a day to sustain her weight. If she reduces her daily intake to 1,500 calories per day, this will result in a weight loss of 0.5 kg (1 lb) per week.

If that same woman exercises every day and burns off another 500 calories, she'll lose 1 kg (about 2 lb) a week. For a man, dropping from 2,500 to 2,000 calories per day will have the same result. Again, exercising will lead to even more! And that's what the Biggest Loser programme aims to achieve.

Keeping to the correct number of portions of each food group per day means that you will hit your calorie target. The healthy eating plan and recipes help you to do this by breaking down your meals into portions. The table opposite is a handy guide to getting the balance right.

What about treats?

Women have an allowance of 100 calories a day for treats and men have 200. For women this could mean a 125 ml (4 fl oz) glass of wine or a small chocolate bar. Men could afford a bottle of lager or two fingers of shortbread. Treats are down to you, but check the calorie counts carefully.

Are you losing weight?

At this level of calorie intake you should be losing weight, but everyone is slightly different. If you are not seeing the weight drop off – and you're not cheating – cut a portion of carbohydrates and fat per day and give it a week to see if that makes a difference. Adjust until you hit the level of portions that gives you a steady weight loss of 1 kg (2 lb) a week.

If the weight is dropping off faster than this, allow yourself an extra portion of protein and carbohydrate, and two extra portions of fruit and veg. Check your weight after a week and adjust if necessary.

DAILY FOOD GROUP PORTIONS

	WOMEN 1,500 KCALS	MEN 2,000 KCALS
CARBOHYDRATES	6 portions	8 portions
FRUIT AND VEG	5 portions	8 portions
PROTEIN	2 portions	3 portions
DAIRY	3 portions	3 portions
FAT AND SUGAR	3 portions	5 portions
TREAT/SNACKS	100 kCals	200 kCals

SUGGESTED MEAL BREAKDOWN

	WOMEN	MEN
BREAKFAST	2 carbs, 1 dairy, 1 fruit	2 carbs, 1 protein, 1 dairy, 2 fruit
LUNCH	2 carbs, 1 protein, 2 veg, 1 dairy	3 carbs, 3 veg, 1 protein, 1 dairy
DINNER	2 carbs, 1 protein, 2 veg, 1 dairy	3 carbs, 3 veg, 1 protein, 1 dairy

Planning your meals

There can be nothing more dispiriting for a dieter than eating the same foods over and over again. Worse still is the thought that you have to stick to a specific diet, with no room to experiment with different flavours, recipes and foods.

The good news is that the Biggest Loser healthy eating plan gives you complete flexibility to eat what you want. You can choose any healthy, nutritious foods, as long as you eat the requisite number of portions each day. If you wise up to the food choices you are making, you do not need to ban any food from your diet. There is no such thing as a bad food, only a bad diet, where the proportions and portion sizes of unhealthy foods are too high.

Following the healthy eating plan is a great opportunity to get back in the kitchen to explore a new approach to cooking and enjoying food. It's also a brilliant way of educating family and friends about making healthy choices, too, so you won't feel like the odd one out at the dinner table.

What about eating out?
If you want to eat out or have the odd ready-meal, simply choose ones that are low in fat and sugar, and make sure that half of your plate is filled with a range of fruit, vegetables or salad. If you head to a Chinese restaurant, stick to boiled rice and steamed fish, chicken or vegetable dishes; similarly, a thin-crust pizza with a vegetable topping can be shared with a friend, with loads of salad on the side. You won't be overdoing the calories and you'll enjoy the treat.

What about drinks?
Water is by far the best drink for anyone wishing to lose weight, and staying hydrated will make you feel fuller, more alert and much more energetic. The more you exercise, the more you should drink. Fruit juice is fine, but it is full of natural sugars that can slow down your weight loss, so stick to one glass a day.

If you are a tea or coffee drinker, choose semi-skimmed or skimmed milk and use sweetener instead of sugar, with the aim of gradually weaning yourself off the need for this sweet kick altogether. Your taste buds are constantly adapting and will get used to the change over time. Non-alcoholic drinks are unlimited, as long as they don't add unnecessary sugar (and calories) to your diet.

Cook smart
Healthy cooking methods include steaming vegetables rather than boiling them, so that their vital nutrients don't leach into the cooking water; using griddles with ridges that allow fat to drain off when you grill meat; and choosing nonstick pans that only need a little oil sprayed on to prevent food from sticking.

	SUGAR	FAT	SATURATES	SALT
WHAT IS HIGH PER 100 G (3½ oz)?	over 15 g	over 20 g	over 5 g	over 1.5 g
WHAT IS MEDIUM PER 100 G (3½ oz)?	between 5 g and 15 g	between 3 g and 20 g	between 1.5 g and 5 g	between 0.3 g and 1.5 g
WHAT IS LOW PER 100 G (3½ oz)?	5 g and below	3 g and below	1.5 g and below	0.3 g and below

Making the right choices

You can choose any healthy, nutritious food, as long as you eat no more than the requisite number of portions each day, and become familiar with what's in the food you are buying. Get into the habit of checking food labels. The handy guide above will help.

Stuck for ideas?

The following pages look at some possible combinations for meals and snacks, for you to try to tempt your tastebuds. Where a page reference is given, this will lead you to the recipe.

Key to the recipes

The recipes on pages 42–81 include both calorie counts per serving and the number of portions of each food group per serving (that's fat/sugar, fruit/veg, protein, carbohydrates and dairy). This, in conjunction with the 'Daily food group portions' chart on page 33, and the 'Six-week healthy eating plan' on pages 36–41 will help you to plan your daily menu. Food group portions are displayed in green circles at the head of each recipe. As your dessert and snack allowance will be measured in terms of calories rather than portions, we haven't included portions on those recipes.

Your six-week healthy eating plan

Week one

	Monday	Tuesday	Wednesday	Thursday	Friday	Saturday	Sunday
Breakfast	Wholegrain toast with light cream cheese and sliced tomatoes	Porridge with milk and banana	Poached eggs on wholemeal toast	Swiss-style muesli with fruit and yogurt	Low-fat natural yogurt with fruit	Sesame-seed bagel with light cream cheese and smoked salmon	Scrambled eggs on wholegrain toast with grilled tomatoes and mushrooms
Lunch	Tuna, rice and vegetable salad	Couscous, roasted vegetable and feta cheese salad	Baked potato with reduced-sugar baked beans	Wholemeal pitta bread with hummus (see page 81) and salad	Chicken pasta salad with a light lemon vinaigrette	Homemade thin-crust vegetable pizza with salad	Smoked mackerel salad with crusty bread
Dinner	Homemade fish fingers with baked potato and salad	Chicken, cashew and vegetable stir-fry with noodles	Homemade burgers in a wholemeal bun with salad	Lean steak with baked sweet potato and vegetables	Baked trout with bulgar wheat (see page 68) with steamed vegetables	Low-fat Thai green curry with prawns and brown rice	Chicken pasta with roasted vegetables
Extras	Fresh fruit slices Low-fat fruit yogurt	Hummus (see page 81) with vegetable batons Fat-free frozen yogurt	Handful of seeds or nuts Homemade fruit crumble	Air-popped plain popcorn Sliced mango with raspberries	Two oatcakes with 1 tsp peanut butter Mixed berries	Red pepper and spring onion dip (see page 81) with vegetable batons Sugar-free jelly	Mango and passion-fruit brûlée (see page 76)

Week two

	Monday	Tuesday	Wednesday	Thursday	Friday	Saturday	Sunday
Breakfast	Porridge with milk and dried apricots	Sesame-seed bagel with light cream cheese and smoked salmon	Poached eggs on wholemeal toast	Pumpkin seed and apricot muesli (see page 46)	Low-fat natural yogurt with low-sugar fruit compote	Lean grilled bacon with wholemeal toast and sliced tomatoes	Pancakes with fresh fruit and yogurt
Lunch	Baked potato with low-fat cottage cheese	Baked sweet potato with chicken (see page 57)	Tuna pasta salad with sweetcorn and spring onions	Chicken salad sandwich on wholegrain bread with low-fat mayonnaise	Roasted vegetable and feta cheese wrap	Chickpea and tomato soup (see page 52) with a wholegrain bun	Roast chicken salad with grilled peppers and courgettes
Dinner	Spaghetti Bolognese with salad	Homemade lasagne with vegetables	Grilled trout with steamed vegetables and brown rice	Pork, vegetable and noodle stir-fry	Baked salmon with steamed vegetables and new potatoes	Chicken with pesto and veggie mash (see page 70)	Sea bass with tomato and basil sauce (see page 69)
Extras	Hummus (see page 81) with vegetable batons Baked bananas	Fresh fruit slices Low-fat chocolate mousse	Red pepper with light cream cheese Baked pineapple	Low-fat cheese Blueberry and lemon ice cream (see page 77)	Fresh fruit slices Strawberries with 2 squares of melted dark chocolate	Handful of nuts or seeds Sugar-free jelly with berries	Air-popped plain popcorn Sliced mango with raspberries

Week three

	Monday	Tuesday	Wednesday	Thursday	Friday	Saturday	Sunday
Breakfast	Wholemeal English muffins with scrambled eggs	Orange smoothie (see page 44)	Summer fruits with honeyed oats (see page 45)	Porridge with apricot purée (see page 48)	Breakfast cereal bars (see page 47)	Herby scrambled eggs on rye (see page 49)	Pancakes with fresh fruit and yogurt
Lunch	Prawn, vegetable and rice salad	Wholemeal pitta with hummus (see page 81) and roasted vegetables	Puy lentil and goats' cheese salad (see page 56)	Homemade thin-crust vegetable pizza with salad	Pasta salad with crab and rocket (see page 59)	Grilled tuna steak with new potatoes and vegetables	Tomato and basil soup with a wholemeal roll
Dinner	Roasted butternut squash with feta cheese and pumpkin seeds with green beans	Thai noodles with tofu (see page 62)	Baked haddock with baked sweet potatoes and vegetables	Roast chicken with roasted vegetables and baked potato	Baked salmon with bulgar wheat and vegetables	Yellow split pea and pepper patties (see page 65)	Thai beef and mixed-pepper stir-fry (see page 72) with coconut rice
Extras	Nectarine and blueberry tartlets (see page 75)	Air-popped plain popcorn Sugar-free jelly with berries	Fresh fruit slices Low-fat crème caramel	Carrots with homemade tzatziki (see page 65) Strawberry crush (see page 78)	Two rice cakes with 1 tsp low-fat almond butter Fresh pineapple	Handful of nuts or seeds Sliced papaya	Hummus (see page 81) with vegetable batons Roasted peaches

Week four

	Monday	Tuesday	Wednesday	Thursday	Friday	Saturday	Sunday
Breakfast	Grilled bacon medallions, tomatoes and mushrooms on wholemeal toast	Low-fat natural yogurt with fruit	Porridge with milk and banana	Wholemeal English muffins with scrambled eggs	Raspberry and strawberry smoothie (see page 42)	Summer fruits with honeyed oats (see page 45)	Mushroom omelette (see page 50) with a wholegrain roll
Lunch	Chicken Caesar salad (see page 53)	Homemade thin-crust vegetable pizza with salad	Couscous, roasted vegetable and feta cheese salad	Baked potato with reduced-sugar baked beans	Greek salad bruschetta with sardines (see page 58)	Smoked mackerel salad with crusty bread	New potato, and bacon salad (see page 54)
Dinner	Homemade fish fingers with baked potato and salad	Low-fat Thai green curry with prawns and brown rice	Salmon fishcakes (see page 67) with steamed green beans	Bolognese-filled pasta shells (see page 66)	Vegetable curry (see page 63)	Homemade burgers in a wholemeal bun with salad	Roast chicken with steamed vegetables and rice
Extras	Hummus (see page 81) with vegetable batons Fat-free frozen yogurt	Oatcakes with 1 tsp peanut butter Fresh raspberries	Carrots with homemade tzatziki (see page 65) Low-fat chocolate mousse	Fresh fruit slices Strawberry crush (see page 78)	Handful of nuts or seeds Mango and passion-fruit brûlée (see page 76)	Red pepper and spring onion dip (see page 81) with vegetable batons	Fresh fruit slices Low-fat frozen yogurt

Week five

	Monday	Tuesday	Wednesday	Thursday	Friday	Saturday	Sunday
Breakfast	Herby scrambled eggs on rye (see page 49)	Low-fat natural yogurt with fruit compote	Raspberry and strawberry smoothie (see page 42)	Pumpkin seed and apricot muesli (see page 46)	Wholegrain bread with light cream cheese and sliced tomatoes	Poached eggs on wholegrain toast	Porridge with apricot purée (see page 48)
Lunch	Baked potato with low-fat cottage cheese and ham	Chicken pasta salad with a light lemon vinaigrette	New potato and bacon salad (see page 54)	Tomato and basil soup with a wholemeal roll	Prawn, mango & avocado wrap (see page 60)	Chicken Caesar salad (see page 53)	Goats' cheese and pine nut salad with a crusty roll
Dinner	Homemade burgers served in a bun with salad	Baked trout with bulgar wheat (see page 68) with steamed vegetables	Steak with baked sweet potato and vegetables	Salmon fishcakes (see page 67) with steamed green beans	Chicken with roasted vegetables and new potatoes	Spaghetti Bolognese with salad	Sea bass with tomato and basil sauce (see page 69)
Extras	Sliced mango and raspberries	Red pepper and spring onion dip (see page 81) with vegetable batons	Handful of nuts or seeds Low-fat chocolate mousse	Low-fat cheese Two squares of dark chocolate	Blueberry and lemon ice cream (see page 77)	Air-popped plain popcorn Low-fat yogurt	Mango and passion-fruit brûlée (see page 76)

Week six

	Monday	Tuesday	Wednesday	Thursday	Friday	Saturday	Sunday
Breakfast	Wholegrain bread with light cream cheese and sliced tomatoes	Poached eggs on wholemeal toast	Orange smoothie (see page 44)	Porridge with apricot purée (see page 48)	Sesame-seed bagel with light cream cheese and smoked salmon	Mushroom omelette (see page 50) with a wholegrain roll	Pancakes with fresh fruit and yogurt
Lunch	Tomato and basil soup with a wholemeal roll	Puy lentil and goats' cheese salad (see page 56)	Chicken pasta salad with a light lemon vinaigrette	Chickpea and tomato soup (see page 52)	Prawn, vegetable and rice salad	Prawn, mango and avocado wrap (see page 60)	Baked sweet potato with chicken (see page 57)
Dinner	Baked haddock with rice and vegetables	Chicken with pesto and veggie mash (see page 70)	Yellow split pea and pepper patties (see page 65)	Salmon fishcakes (see page 67) with steamed green beans	Bolognese-filled pasta shells (see page 66)	Roasted butternut squash with feta cheese and pumpkin seeds with green beans	Cod with tomato sauce and rice
Extras	Handful of nuts or seeds Fresh fruit slices	Low-fat fruit yogurt Sugar-free jelly with berries	Fresh fruit slices Mango and passion-fruit brûlée (see page 76)	Sliced mango with raspberries	Hummus (see page 81) with vegetable batons Mixed berries with low-fat yogurt	Oatcakes with 1 tsp peanut butter Homemade fruit crumble	Air-popped plain popcorn Nectarine and blueberry tartlets (see page 75)

FAT/SUGAR   **2½** FRUIT/VEG   **0** PROTEIN   **0** CARBOHYDRATES   **½** DAIRY

Raspberry & strawberry smoothie

Smoothies are a healthy breakfast option, but it's important to keep track of your fruit portions as even fruit, if eaten in large quantities, can lead to excess calorie intake.

Calories 146 kCals

Serves 4

4 oranges
2 apples
160 g (5¾ oz) raspberries, fresh
  or frozen
160 g (5¾ oz) strawberries, fresh
  or frozen
300 g (10 oz) low-fat natural
  yogurt

1   Juice the oranges and apples, then whizz the juice in a blender with the raspberries, strawberries and yogurt. Serve immediately.

TWISTS & VARIATIONS

Any fresh or frozen berries will work well here, including blackberries, blueberries and pitted summer cherries. Add the zest of half an orange for an extra kick.

0 FAT/SUGAR   **3** FRUIT/VEG   **0** PROTEIN   **0** CARBOHYDRATES   **0** DAIRY

Orange smoothie

The carrots in this nutritious breakfast smoothie give it a vivid orange colour, a smooth taste and a good kick of vitamins. A great way to start the day!

Calories 163 kCals

Serves 4

4 large carrots
4 oranges
400 g (13 oz) banana
4 fresh or ready-to-eat dried apricots

1   Juice the carrots and oranges. Whizz the juice in a blender with the banana, apricots and a few ice cubes. Serve immediately.

TWISTS & VARIATIONS

Swap the banana for half a small avocado, which will give a creamy texture and lots of vitamin E.

2 FAT/SUGAR   **2½** FRUIT/VEG   **1** PROTEIN   **0** CARBOHYDRATES   **0** DAIRY

Summer fruits with honeyed oats

This fruity breakfast crumble also makes an easy, satisfying dessert and is a delicious way to reach your daily fruit intake – and it will keep you feeling full until lunchtime!

Calories 309 kCals

Serves 4

16 apricots, pitted and halved
16 strawberries, hulled and halved
4 tablespoons fat-free Greek
   yogurt
4 dessertspoons clear honey
4 tablespoons rolled oats
100 g (3½ oz) toasted almonds

1   Divide the apricots and strawberries between four bowls. Add the Greek yogurt and honey and sprinkle the oats and almonds over the top.

0 FAT/SUGAR **2** FRUIT/VEG **1** PROTEIN **2** CARBOHYDRATES **0** DAIRY

Pumpkin seed & apricot muesli

Loaded with healthy fats and juicy, fresh fruits, this delicious muesli is head and shoulders above any store-bought varieties.

Calories 339 kCals

Serves 4

200 g (7 oz) rolled jumbo oats
2 tablespoons sultanas or raisins
2 tablespoons pumpkin or
  sunflower seeds
2 tablespoons chopped almonds
50 g (2 oz) ready-to-eat dried
  apricots, chopped
4 tablespoons orange or apple juice
4 small apples, peeled and grated
6 tablespoons skimmed milk or
  soya milk

1   Divide the oats, sultanas or raisins, seeds, almonds and apricots between four bowls, then add the fruit juice.

2   Add the grated apples and stir to mix. Top with your chosen milk and serve.

TWISTS & VARIATIONS

If you're not a morning person, make this muesli the night before. Carry out step 1 and put the mixture in the refrigerator overnight. The next morning, add the apples and milk. This will also give a softer-textured muesli.

FAT/SUGAR FRUIT/VEG PROTEIN ① CARBOHYDRATES ⓪ DAIRY

Breakfast cereal bars

These nutritious, delicious breakfast bars are great for breakfast on the run or a quick snack. They'll last for up to a week in an air-tight container.

Calories 299 kCals

Serves 4

50 g (2 oz) low-fat margarine
15 g (½ oz) light muscovado sugar
1 tablespoon golden syrup
60 g (2¼ oz) millet flakes
25 g (1 oz) quinoa
25 g (1 oz) dried cherries or cranberries
40 g (1½ oz) sultanas
15 g (½ oz) sunflower seeds
15 g (½ oz) sesame seeds
15 g (½ oz) linseeds
25 g (1 oz) unsweetened desiccated coconut
1 egg, lightly beaten

1 Grease a 16.5 x 10 cm (6½ x 4 inch) shallow rectangular baking tin. Beat together the margarine, sugar and syrup until creamy.

2 Add all of the remaining ingredients and beat well until combined. Turn into the tin and level the surface with the back of a metal spoon.

3 Bake in a preheated oven, 180°C (350°F), Gas Mark 4, for 35 minutes until a deep golden colour. Leave to cool in the tin.

4 Turn out on to a wooden board and carefully cut into 8 fingers using a serrated knife.

TWISTS & VARIATIONS

For tropical cereal bars, prepare the recipe as above, replacing the dried cherries or cranberries with 50 g (2 oz) finely chopped dried pineapple and replacing the sultanas with 75 g (3 oz) dried mango.

½ FAT/SUGAR   2 FRUIT/VEG   **0** PROTEIN   **2** CARBOHYDRATES   **1** DAIRY

Porridge with apricot purée

This hearty, filling porridge, served with homemade apricot purée, will provide a sustained source of energy to keep you going all morning.

Calories 375 kCals

Serves 4

200 g (7 oz) rolled oats
800 ml (1⅓ pints) skimmed milk
2 teaspoons soft brown sugar
175 g (6 oz) ready-to-eat dried apricots
300 ml (½ pint) orange juice

1   Place the oats, milk and sugar in a saucepan and bring to the boil. Reduce the heat and simmer for about 10 minutes until the oats are softened and the required consistency is reached.

2   Meanwhile, place the apricots and orange juice in a separate saucepan and bring to the boil. Reduce the heat and simmer for 10 minutes. Transfer to a food processor or blender and process until smooth. Serve the purée stirred into the porridge.

TWISTS & VARIATIONS

Dried mangoes, blueberries and even sour cherries make a delicious purée, instead of apricots. Sprinkle your porridge with fresh fruit or a little cinnamon for extra flavour.

0 FAT/SUGAR **1** FRUIT/VEG **1** PROTEIN **1** CARBOHYDRATES **¼** DAIRY

Herby scrambled eggs on rye

Not only a tasty, low-fat, protein-rich breakfast, these eggs are so delicious and satisfying you'll want them for lunch … and dinner, too!

Calories 283 kCals

Serves 4

8 eggs
4 tablespoons semi-skimmed milk
4 teaspoons low-fat margarine
2 tablespoons light cream cheese
2 tablespoons chopped mixed herbs (such as parsley, oregano and chives)
salt, if liked, and black pepper

To serve
4 medium slices of rye bread
28 cherry tomatoes, grilled

1 In a bowl, beat the eggs and milk together and season with salt, if liked, and black pepper. Heat the margarine in a nonstick frying pan, add the egg mixture and stir constantly with a wooden spoon for a few minutes until the eggs are softly set.

2 Remove the pan from the heat and stir in the cream cheese and herbs, then serve on slices of rye bread, accompanied by the grilled cherry tomatoes.

TWISTS & VARIATIONS
Instead of light cream cheese, why not use light ricotta or crumbled feta? For an extra treat, serve with a small slice of smoked salmon.

1 FAT/SUGAR   ½ FRUIT/VEG   1 PROTEIN   1 CARBOHYDRATES   ¼ DAIRY

Mushroom omelette

This fragrant, appetizing omelette makes an ideal brunch for weekends or can be eaten as a light supper and served alongside a fresh green salad.

Calories **258 kCals**

Serves **4**

2 tablespoons low-fat margarine
**200 g (7 oz) mushrooms, trimmed
and sliced**
8 eggs, beaten
2 tablespoons chopped parsley
50 g (2 oz) Gruyère cheese, grated
black pepper
4 wholegrain rolls, to serve

1 Melt a little of the margarine in a nonstick frying pan, add the mushrooms and sauté for 5–6 minutes until cooked and any moisture has evaporated. Remove the mushrooms from the pan.

2 Melt a little more margarine in the same pan and add one-quarter of the beaten egg. Season well with black pepper and stir with a wooden spoon, bringing the cooked egg to the centre of the pan and allowing the runny egg to flow to the edge of the pan and cook.

3 When there is only a little liquid egg left, sprinkle over a few mushrooms and some of the parsley and Gruyère. Fold the omelette over, tip on to a warm serving plate and keep warm while you make 3 more omelettes in the same way. Serve each omelette with a wholegrain roll.

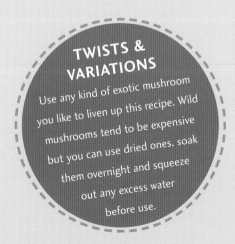

TWISTS & VARIATIONS

Use any kind of exotic mushroom you like to liven up this recipe. Wild mushrooms tend to be expensive but you can use dried ones, soak them overnight and squeeze out any excess water before use.

PERFECT PORTIONS
To balance this meal, serve with a fresh green salad or follow it with a piece of fruit.

1 FAT/SUGAR　　**2** FRUIT/VEG　　**1** PROTEIN　　**2** CARBOHYDRATES　　**0** DAIRY

Chickpea & tomato soup

This light soup is bursting with vitamins, minerals and protein. Serve it with a crusty mixed grain roll to get your carbohydrates, and you'll have a perfectly balanced meal.

Calories 429 kCals

Serves 4

4 teaspoons olive oil
1 onion, roughly chopped
1 garlic clove, crushed
1 carrot, roughly chopped
**1 red pepper, cored, deseeded and
　roughly chopped**
1 teaspoon cumin seeds
500 ml (17 fl oz) vegetable stock
**400 g (13 oz) can chopped
　tomatoes**
**20 g (¾ oz) each pumpkin, sesame
　and sunflower seeds**
**410 g (13½ oz) can chickpeas,
　drained and rinsed**
**2 tablespoons chopped fresh
　coriander**
salt and black pepper
4 crusty mixed grain rolls, to serve

1　Heat the oil in a large saucepan over medium heat, add the onion, garlic, carrot, red pepper and cumin seeds and stir-fry for about 1 minute. Add the stock and tomatoes and simmer for 5 minutes until the vegetables are soft.

2　Meanwhile, dry-fry the seeds in a pan over medium heat until they are golden. Set aside to cool.

3　Remove the vegetable pan from the heat and use a hand-held blender to purée the vegetables. Alternatively, mash them by hand. Stir through the chickpeas and heat through for 2 minutes.

4　Season to taste, sprinkle over the toasted seeds and fresh coriander and serve with crusty mixed grain rolls.

0 FAT/SUGAR   **1** FRUIT/VEG   **1** PROTEIN   **1** CARBOHYDRATES   **0** DAIRY

Chicken Caesar salad

Fresher, lighter and tastier than a traditional Caesar salad, this lunch dish provides an excellent source of protein and surprisingly little fat.

Calories 333 kCals

Serves 4

4 small boneless, skinless chicken breasts
2 tablespoons olive oil
2 cos lettuces, chopped
1 cucumber, sliced
2 green peppers, cored, deseeded and sliced into strips
8 spring onions, finely sliced

Croûtons

4 medium slices of wholegrain bread
2 garlic cloves, halved

Dressing

3 tablespoons light crème fraîche
1 anchovy fillet, chopped
grated rind and juice of ½ lemon
2 tablespoons freshly grated Parmesan cheese
salt, if liked, and black pepper

1 Brush the chicken breasts with a little of the oil and season well with black pepper. Heat a griddle until hot, place the chicken breasts on the griddle and cook for 3–4 minutes on each side until cooked through. Slice each chicken breast.

2 Divide the lettuce, cucumber, peppers and spring onions between 4 plates and top each with a sliced chicken breast.

3 To make the croûtons, drizzle the remaining oil over the bread and grill until toasted on each side. Rub all over with the cut sides of the garlic, cut the toast into cubes and add to the salad.

4 Blend all the dressing ingredients together and drizzle over the salad. Serve immediately.

PERFECT PORTIONS
To balance this meal, follow it with a piece of fruit.

FAT/SUGAR FRUIT/VEG PROTEIN  CARBOHYDRATES DAIRY

New potato & bacon salad

This simple salad is a good source of healthy carbohydrates, protein and vegetables, and is so full of flavour that it is sure to become a staple in your lunchbox.

Calories 299 kCals

Serves 4

**800 g (1 lb 12 oz) baby new
  potatoes, scrubbed
8 lean back bacon rashers, chopped
2 tablespoons olive oil
1 teaspoon Dijon mustard
4 tablespoons lemon juice
1 teaspoon clear honey
150 g (5 oz) watercress, roughly
  chopped
150 g (5 oz) rocket leaves
2 heads of red chicory or
  radicchio, cut into bite-sized
  pieces
black pepper**

1   Cook the potatoes in a saucepan of boiling water for 12–15 minutes until tender. Drain and tip into a serving bowl.

2   Cook the bacon in a dry, nonstick pan for 3–4 minutes until crisp. Add the oil, mustard, lemon juice and honey and stir well. Tip into the bowl with the potatoes, mix together and set aside for 30 minutes.

3   Stir through the remaining ingredients and season well with black pepper. Serve immediately.

PERFECT PORTIONS
To balance this meal, follow it with a piece of fruit.

0 FAT/SUGAR   **1** FRUIT/VEG   **1** PROTEIN   **2** CARBOHYDRATES   **1** DAIRY

Puy lentil & goats' cheese salad

Rich with Eastern flavours, this satisfying salad provides a healthy source of protein and other key nutrients to keep you going all afternoon.

Calories 530 kCals

Serves 4

2 teaspoons olive oil
2 teaspoons cumin seeds
2 garlic cloves, crushed
2 teaspoons grated fresh root ginger
200 g (7 oz) Puy lentils
750 ml (1 ¼ pints) vegetable stock
2 tablespoons chopped mint
2 tablespoons fresh chopped coriander
½ lime
325 g (11 oz) baby spinach leaves
160 g (5¾ oz) goats' cheese, crumbled
salt and black pepper
8 medium slices granary bread, to serve

1 Heat the oil in a saucepan over medium heat, add the cumin seeds, garlic and ginger and cook for 1 minute. Add the lentils and cook for a further minute.

2 Add the stock to the pan, stir and simmer for 25 minutes, until all the liquid is absorbed and the lentils are tender. Check the seasoning. Remove the pan from the heat and set aside to cool. Stir in the mint and coriander and add a squeeze of lime.

3 Arrange the spinach leaves in four individual bowls, top with a quarter of the lentils and the goats' cheese, season with black pepper and serve with slices of granary bread.

PERFECT PORTIONS
To balance this meal, follow it with a piece of fruit.

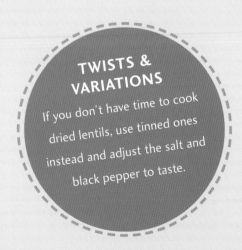

TWISTS & VARIATIONS
If you don't have time to cook dried lentils, use tinned ones instead and adjust the salt and black pepper to taste.

FAT/SUGAR   FRUIT/VEG   PROTEIN   CARBOHYDRATES   ½ DAIRY

Baked sweet potato with chicken

The fat content of this dish is very low, but the herbs make it rich in flavour.

Next time you fancy a baked potato for lunch, opt for this healthier alternative.

Calories 304 kCals

Serves 4

4 sweet potatoes, about 200 g (7 oz) each
4 boneless, skinless chicken breasts
6 tablespoons chopped mixed herbs (such as mint, parsley, fresh coriander and oregano)
1 garlic clove
1 tablespoon capers
2 teaspoons clear honey
1 tablespoon Dijon mustard
1 tablespoon olive oil
4 tablespoons light cream cheese
black pepper
16 florets of broccoli, steamed, to serve

1   Place the potatoes on a baking sheet and cook in a preheated oven, 200°C (400°F), Gas Mark 6, for 1–1¼ hours until tender.

2   Meanwhile, cut 3 slices into the flesh of each chicken breast (be careful you don't cut all the way through). Place the herbs, garlic, capers, honey, mustard and a little of the oil in a food processor or blender and process until well combined. Rub this mixture over the chicken, cover and leave in the refrigerator for at least 30 minutes to allow the flavours to develop.

3   Heat a griddle until hot, drizzle the remaining oil over the chicken, then place the chicken on the griddle and cook for 3–4 minutes on each side until beginning to char and the chicken is cooked through.

4   Cut the sweet potatoes open, spoon in some cream cheese and season with plenty of black pepper. Serve topped with the chicken and accompanied by the steamed broccoli.

2 FAT/SUGAR   **1** FRUIT/VEG   **1** PROTEIN  **2** CARBOHYDRATES   **1** DAIRY

Greek salad bruschetta with sardines

Sardines are an oily fish containing essential omega-3 fatty acids that are important for the health of your heart. Low in calories, they are a great healthy-eating option.

Calories 561 kCals

Serves 4

4 medium slices of ciabatta bread
1 tablespoon olive oil
1 garlic clove, halved
4 x 125 g (4 oz) cans sardines

Greek salad

4 tomatoes, each cut into 8 pieces
½ cucumber, deseeded and cut
  into 1 cm (½ inch) chunks
12 pitted black olives, halved
160 g (5¾ oz) feta cheese,
  cut into 1 cm (½ inch) cubes
1 tablespoon lemon juice
2 tablespoons olive oil
10 mint leaves, finely shredded
salt and black pepper

1 Combine all the Greek salad ingredients and season with salt and black pepper.

2 Drizzle the slices of ciabatta with the oil and place on a hot griddle or under a hot grill. Cook for 2–3 minutes each side to toast. When they are toasted, rub both sides with the cut sides of garlic.

3 Top the ciabatta with the Greek salad and the sardines.

PERFECT PORTIONS
To balance this meal, follow it with a piece of fruit.

FAT/SUGAR · FRUIT/VEG · PROTEIN · 2 CARBOHYDRATES · 0 DAIRY

Pasta salad with crab & rocket

This surprisingly flavourful pasta salad is ideal for packed lunches and picnics. Smaller portions will make a well-balanced snack, too.

Calories 334 kCals

Serves 4

200 g (7 oz) dried pasta (such as penne)
grated rind and juice of 2 limes
8 tablespoons half-fat crème fraîche
480 g (17 oz) canned crab meat, drained
28 cherry tomatoes, halved
4 generous handfuls of rocket leaves

1   Cook the pasta according to the instructions on the packet. Rinse and leave to cool.

2   In a large bowl mix together the lime rind and juice, crème fraîche and crab meat. Add the pasta and mix again.

3   Add the tomatoes and rocket to the bowl, toss everything together and serve.

TWISTS & VARIATIONS
Choose wholegrain or spelt pasta for added nutritional value – and fibre. Tuna works well in place of the crab, too.

FAT/SUGAR FRUIT/VEG PROTEIN  CARBOHYDRATES DAIRY

Prawn, mango & avocado wrap

These beautiful little wraps taste as good as they look, and contain plenty of protein and vitamins for optimum nutrition.

Calories 327 kCals

Serves 4

3 tablespoons half-fat crème fraîche
3 teaspoons tomato ketchup
Tabasco sauce, to taste
300 g (10 oz) cooked peeled prawns
1 mango, peeled and thinly sliced
1 avocado, peeled and sliced
4 flour tortillas
100 g (3½ oz) watercress
black pepper

1 In a medium bowl mix together the crème fraîche and ketchup. Add a few drops of Tabasco sauce to taste.

2 Add the prawns, mango and avocado and toss the mixture together. Divide the mixture between the tortillas, add some watercress, season with black pepper, roll them up and serve immediately.

3 If you're taking this recipe to work, don't make up the wrap until lunchtime or it will be too soggy to eat. Instead, put the prawn mixture in an airtight container, place it in a refrigerator when you get to work, and then construct the tortilla when you are ready to eat it.

TWISTS & VARIATIONS

Crayfish and white crab meat can be substituted for the prawns or blended together for a seafood cocktail.

PERFECT PORTIONS
To balance this meal, follow it with a piece of fruit.

1 FAT/SUGAR   **1½** FRUIT/VEG   **1** PROTEIN   **2** CARBOHYDRATES   **0** DAIRY

Thai noodles with tofu

This fragrant noodle dish is bursting with flavour and healthy vegetarian protein.
If you don't like tofu, substitute 125 g (4 oz) of chicken per person.

Calories 411 kCals

Serves 4

500 g (1 lb) tofu, diced
3 tablespoons dark soy sauce
2 teaspoons grated lime rind
2 litres (3½ pints) vegetable stock
3 slices of fresh root ginger
2 garlic cloves
2 fresh coriander sprigs
3 lemon grass stalks, crushed
1 red chilli, bruised
200 g (7 oz) dried egg noodles
125 g (4 oz) button mushrooms,
  sliced
2 large carrots, cut into matchsticks
125 g (4 oz) sugar snap peas
125 g (4 oz) Chinese cabbage,
  shredded
2 tablespoons chopped fresh
  coriander

1   Put the tofu in a shallow dish with the soy sauce and lime rind. Marinate for 30 minutes.

2   Meanwhile, put the vegetable stock into a large saucepan and add the ginger, garlic, coriander sprigs, lemon grass and chilli. Bring to the boil, reduce the heat, cover and simmer for 30 minutes.

3   Strain the vegetable stock into another saucepan, return to the boil and plunge in the noodles. Add the sliced mushrooms and marinated tofu with any remaining marinade. Reduce the heat and simmer gently for 4 minutes.

4   Stir in the carrots, sugar snap peas, Chinese cabbage and chopped coriander, cook for a further 3–4 minutes. Serve immediately.

2½ FAT/SUGAR   3 FRUIT/VEG   1 PROTEIN    2 CARBOHYDRATES   0 DAIRY

Vegetable curry

Rich and delicious, this curry is bursting with vitamin-packed vegetables and pulses, and is the perfect low-fat addition to your healthy eating programme.

Calories 622 kCals

Serves 4

2 teaspoons olive oil
1 onion, chopped
1 garlic clove, crushed
2 tablespoons medium curry paste
750 g (1½ lb) prepared vegetables (such as courgettes, peppers and squash), cut into even-sized pieces
2 x 410 g (13½ oz) cans mixed pulses, drained and rinsed
400 g (13 oz) can chopped tomatoes
400 g (13 oz) can reduced-fat coconut milk
2 tablespoons chopped fresh coriander
200 g (7 oz) brown rice, cooked according to packet instructions, to serve

1 Heat the oil in a large saucepan then add the onion and garlic and fry for 2 minutes. Stir in the curry paste and fry for 1 minute more.

2 Add the vegetables and mixed pulses and fry for 2–3 minutes, stirring occasionally, then add the tomatoes and coconut milk. Stir well, bring to the boil then lower the heat and simmer for 12–15 minutes or until all the vegetables are cooked. Stir in the coriander and serve immediately, accompanied by the rice.

TWISTS & VARIATIONS

Any combination of vegetables works well in this dish, including frozen mixed vegetables – perfect if you are in a hurry!

0 FAT/SUGAR   **1** FRUIT/VEG   **1** PROTEIN   **0** CARBOHYDRATES   **½** DAIRY

Yellow split pea & pepper patties

These protein-rich patties are ideal for lunch or dinner – or as a starter for a casual dinner party. Split peas are a worthwhile addition to a nutritious and healthy diet.

Calories 411 kCals

Serves 4

3 garlic cloves
200 g (7 oz) yellow split peas
950 ml (32 fl oz) vegetable stock
olive oil spray
2 red peppers, halved, cored and deseeded
1 yellow pepper, halved, cored and deseeded
1 red onion, quartered
1 tablespoon chopped fresh mint
2 tablespoons capers, rinsed and chopped
salt and pepper

Tzatziki

½ cucumber, finely chopped
1 garlic clove, crushed
2 tablespoons chopped fresh mint
300ml (½ pint) low-fat yogurt
fresh mint leaves, to garnish

1   Peel and halve a garlic clove and cook it with the split peas in the stock for 40–45 minutes, until the split peas are tender, starting to break down and the water is absorbed, adding a little more water if necessary. Check the seasoning and leave to cool completely.

2   Meanwhile, make the tzatziki. Combine the cucumber with the garlic, mint and yogurt, and garnish with mint leaves.

3   Next, lightly spray a roasting tin with oil. Put the remaining unpeeled garlic cloves in the tin with the peppers and onion and cook in a preheated oven, 200°C (400°F), Gas Mark 6, for 20 minutes. Squeeze the roasted garlic cloves from their skins and chop with the roasted vegetables.

4   Mix the split peas with the roasted vegetables, mint and capers, then add salt and black pepper to taste. Using slightly wet hands, squeeze and shape the mixture into patties. Refrigerate until ready to cook.

5   Heat a frying pan and spray with oil. Cook the patties, in batches if necessary, leaving them to cook undisturbed for 2 minutes on each side. Serve either hot or cold, with the tzatziki on the side.

0 FAT/SUGAR   2 FRUIT/VEG   1 PROTEIN   2 CARBOHYDRATES   1 DAIRY

Bolognese-filled pasta shells

A satisfying meal that will appeal to the whole family, these deliciously cheesy pasta shells are lower in calories than you might expect.

Calories **415 kCals**

Serves **4**

1 teaspoon olive oil
1 onion, chopped
1 celery stick, chopped
1 carrot, chopped
200 g (7 oz) mushrooms, sliced
400 g (13 oz) turkey mince
300 ml (½ pint) passata
2 tablespoons chopped parsley
16 large wholewheat pasta shells
100 g (3½ oz) ricotta cheese
2 tablespoons freshly grated
  Parmesan cheese
black pepper
salad, to serve

1   Heat the oil in a large frying pan, add the onion, celery, carrot and mushrooms and fry for 3–4 minutes until softened.

2   Add the turkey mince and continue to fry, stirring to break up, for 5 minutes until browned. Pour the passata over the mince and bring to the boil. Reduce the heat and simmer for 20 minutes. Stir through the parsley and season well with black pepper.

3   Place the pasta shells in a large, ovenproof dish and divide the Bolognese mixture between them. Spoon a little ricotta on top of each, then sprinkle over the Parmesan. Bake in a preheated oven, 200°C (400°F), Gas Mark 6, for 10 minutes until golden and bubbling. Serve with a salad.

TWISTS & VARIATIONS
Try minced beef or chicken in place of the turkey. Cottage cheese works just as well as ricotta.

1 FAT/SUGAR   **1** FRUIT/VEG   **1** PROTEIN   **1½** CARBOHYDRATES   **0** DAIRY

Salmon fishcakes

These little fishcakes make a perfectly balanced Biggest Loser dinner when served with a large portion of healthy steamed green beans.

Calories 359 kCals

Serves 4

400 g (13 oz) new potatoes
grated rind and juice of 1 lemon
3 tablespoons skimmed milk
1 bunch of spring onions, sliced
½ teaspoon cayenne pepper
2 x 200 g (7 oz) cans salmon in
  water or brine, drained, bones
  and skin removed and flaked
2 tablespoons plain flour
1 egg, beaten
75 g (3 oz) fresh white breadcrumbs
4 teaspoons olive oil
salt and black pepper
325 g (11 oz) steamed green
  beans, to serve

1   Cook the potatoes in a pan of lightly salted boiling water until tender. Mash and stir in the lemon rind and juice, milk, spring onions, cayenne pepper and salmon. Season to taste.

2   Place the flour on a small saucer, the beaten egg on another and the breadcrumbs on a third. Form the salmon mixture into 8 patties. Dip each first in the flour, then the egg, and then the breadcrumbs and place on a lightly oiled baking sheet.

3   Drizzle over the remaining oil and cook the fishcakes in a preheated oven at 200°C (400°F), Gas Mark 6, for 12–15 minutes, turning once, until golden and piping hot. Serve with steamed green beans.

0 FAT/SUGAR   2 FRUIT/VEG   1 PROTEIN   2 CARBOHYDRATES   0 DAIRY

Baked trout with bulgar wheat

A simple, fragrant dish, giving you one of your recommended two servings of oily fish a week, this trout is perfect for a summertime dinner party.

Calories 433 kCals

Serves 4

4 trout fillets (100 g/3½ oz each)
handful of chopped dill
3 spring onions, chopped
juice of ½ lemon
200 g (7 oz) bulgar wheat
500 ml (17 fl oz) vegetable stock
2 courgettes, chopped
2 large carrots, grated
2 generous handfuls spinach
salt and black pepper

To garnish
2 tablespoons pine nuts, toasted
orange slices

1   Sprinkle the trout fillets with the dill, spring onions, lemon juice, salt and black pepper. Cover with foil and bake in a preheated oven, 200°C (400°F), Gas Mark 6, for 15–20 minutes.

2   Meanwhile, place the bulgar wheat in a medium saucepan with the stock. Bring to the boil, cover and simmer for 5 minutes. Stir in the courgettes and carrots, cover and simmer for a further 10 minutes, until the water is absorbed. Remove from the heat and stir in the spinach until wilted.

3   Divide the bulgar wheat between 4 plates, top with a trout fillet and garnish with toasted pine nuts and orange slices.

0 FAT/SUGAR   **1** FRUIT/VEG   **1** PROTEIN   **2** CARBOHYDRATES   **0** DAIRY

Sea bass with tomato & basil sauce

This is sea bass with an Italian twist! The tomato and basil complement the light fish perfectly, producing a delicious main meal. Serve with new potatoes and green beans.

Calories 292 kCals

Serves 4

8 plum tomatoes, halved
2 tablespoons lemon juice
grated rind of 1 lemon, plus extra to garnish
4 sea bass fillets, about 150 g (5 oz) each
2 tablespoons chopped basil
4 teaspoons extra virgin olive oil
salt and black pepper

To serve
200 g (7 oz) new potatoes, steamed
320 g (10½ oz) steamed green beans

To garnish
handful of basil leaves
4 lemon wedges

1 Make the sauce up to 2 days in advance. Arrange the tomatoes in a roasting tin, season well and cook in a preheated oven, 200°C (400°F), Gas Mark 6, for 20 minutes.

2 Transfer the tomatoes and any cooking juices to a pan and heat through gently with the lemon juice and rind. Season to taste and set aside until ready to serve.

3 Season the fish fillets and cook under a preheated hot grill for approximately 10 minutes or until the fish is cooked through.

4 Meanwhile, warm the sauce through. Stir the basil and oil through the sauce and spoon it over the fish. Garnish with basil leaves, more grated lemon rind and lemon wedges. Serve accompanied by the steamed new potatoes and green beans.

TWISTS & VARIATIONS

A little fresh thyme and oregano can be added to the sauce to give it even more flavour. Sprinkle fresh leaves on top before serving.

FAT/SUGAR FRUIT/VEG PROTEIN CARBOHYDRATES **0** DAIRY

Chicken with pesto & veggie mash

The root vegetable mash in this recipe is easy to make and the pesto gives it a fantastic flavour. Alongside the chicken, it's a beautifully balanced meal.

Calories 304 kCals

Serves 4

4 boneless, skinless chicken breasts, about 100 g (3½ oz) each
25 g (1 oz) basil leaves
4 teaspoons olive oil
2 tablespoons pine nuts, toasted
1 garlic clove
2 tablespoons grated Parmesan cheese
25 g (1 oz) rocket leaves, plus extra to garnish
400 g (13 oz) potatoes, diced
250 g (8 oz) swede, diced
250 g (8 oz) carrots, diced
salt and black pepper

1   Season the chicken breasts with salt and black pepper.

2   Put the basil, oil, pine nuts, garlic, Parmesan and rocket together in a food processor or blender and process until the mixture is puréed. Set aside.

3   Cook the chicken breasts on a hot griddle for approximately 8–10 minutes, depending on their size, until just cooked through and still succulent.

4   Meanwhile, boil the root vegetables for 12–15 minutes until soft, then mash to a creamy consistency. Swirl the rocket pesto through the mash.

5   Slice each chicken breast diagonally into three pieces and serve alongside the mash. Season with black pepper and garnish with rocket leaves.

FAT/SUGAR   FRUIT/VEG   PROTEIN   CARBOHYDRATES **0** DAIRY

Thai beef & mixed pepper stir-fry

The coconut rice served alongside this delicious stir-fry looks and tastes fattening. But if you use reduced-fat coconut milk, it's not!

Calories 431 kCals

Serves: 4

400 g (13 oz) lean beef fillet
1 tablespoon sesame oil
1 garlic clove, finely chopped
1 lemon grass stalk, finely
  shredded
2.5 cm (1 inch) piece of fresh root
  ginger, peeled and finely chopped
2 red peppers, cored, deseeded
  and thickly sliced
2 green peppers, cored, deseeded
  and thickly sliced
1 onion, thickly sliced
2 tablespoons lime juice
fresh coriander leaves, to garnish
black pepper

Coconut rice

200 g (7 oz) fragrant Thai rice
125 ml (4 fl oz) reduced-fat
  coconut milk

1 Firstly, prepare the coconut rice. Place the rice in a heavy-based pan, pour in the coconut milk and add enough water to come 2.5 cm (1 inch) above the level of the rice. Bring to the boil, then reduce the heat to a slow simmer and cover. Cook for 10 minutes, remove from the heat and keep covered for a further 10 minutes to finish cooking in its own heat.

2 Meanwhile, cut the beef into long, thin strips, cutting across the grain.

3 Heat the oil in a wok or large frying pan over a high heat. Add the garlic and stir-fry for 1 minute. Add the beef and stir-fry for 2–3 minutes until lightly coloured. Stir in the lemon grass and ginger and remove the pan from the heat. Remove the beef from the pan and set aside.

4 Add the peppers and onion to the pan and stir-fry for 2–3 minutes until the onions are just turning golden brown and are slightly softened.

5 Return the beef to the pan, stir in the lime juice and season to taste with black pepper.

6 Fluff up the coconut rice with a fork and serve alongside the stir-fry.

Nectarine & blueberry tartlets

These exquisite, fruity little tarts are light and delicious – and impressive enough to be served to even the most discerning of guests!

Calories 166 kCals

Serves 4

sunflower oil, for brushing
4 sheets of filo pastry (thawed if frozen), each 30 x 18 cm (12 x 7 inches)
2 tablespoons low-sugar red berry jam
juice of ½ orange
4 ripe nectarines, halved, pitted and sliced
150 g (5 oz) blueberries

1 Lightly oil the sheets of filo pastry and cut each into 6 pieces, 10 x 9 cm (4 x 3½ inches). Arrange a piece of filo in each of the sections of a deep, lightly oiled, 12-hole muffin tin. Add a second piece at a slight angle to the first to give a pretty, jagged edge to each pastry case.

2 Bake the pastry cases in a preheated oven, 180°C (350°F), Gas Mark 4, for 6–8 minutes until golden.

3 Meanwhile, warm the jam and orange juice in a large saucepan, add the nectarines and blueberries and warm through.

4 Carefully lift the tartlet cases out of the muffin tin and transfer them to serving dishes. Fill with the warm fruits and serve.

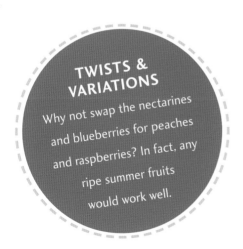

TWISTS & VARIATIONS

Why not swap the nectarines and blueberries for peaches and raspberries? In fact, any ripe summer fruits would work well.

Mango & passion-fruit brûlée

These little brûlées taste as sinful as they look, but made with low-fat yogurt and crème fraîche, they won't blow your daily calorie totals.

Calories 180 kCals

Serves 4

1 small mango, peeled, stoned and thinly sliced
2 passion-fruit, flesh scooped out
300 g (10 oz) low-fat natural yogurt
200 ml (7 fl oz) half-fat crème fraîche
1 tablespoon icing sugar
few drops of vanilla essence
2 tablespoons demerara sugar

1   Divide the mango slices equally between 4 ramekins.

2   Stir together the passion-fruit flesh, yogurt, crème fraîche, icing sugar and vanilla essence, and spoon the mixture over the mango. Tap the ramekins to give the contents a flat surface.

3   Sprinkle over the demerara sugar and cook under a preheated hot grill for 1–2 minutes until the sugar is melted. Chill for 30 minutes before serving.

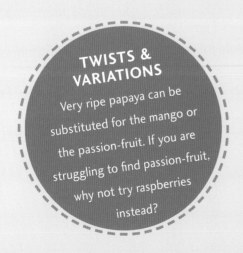

TWISTS & VARIATIONS

Very ripe papaya can be substituted for the mango or the passion-fruit. If you are struggling to find passion-fruit, why not try raspberries instead?

Blueberry & lemon ice cream

Ice cream when watching your weight? It's true! Fresh and fruity, this dessert is bursting with nutrient-rich berries and zesty lemon. A real treat!

Calories 258 kCals

Serves 4

500 g (1 lb) frozen blueberries
500 g (1 lb) fat-free Greek yogurt
125 g (4 oz) icing sugar, plus extra
** to decorate**
grated rind of 2 lemons
1 tablespoon lemon juice

1 Reserve a few blueberries for decoration. Put the remainder of the blueberries in a food processor or blender with the yogurt, icing sugar and lemon rind and juice and process until smooth.

2 Spoon the mixture into a 600 ml (1 pint) freezerproof container and freeze.

3 Eat when the frozen yogurt is softly frozen and easily spoonable. Before serving, decorate with the reserved blueberries and a sprinkling of icing sugar. Use within 3 days.

TWISTS & VARIATIONS
Frozen raspberries or blackberries can be used in place of blueberries – or why not try a blend?

Strawberry crush

This pretty, low-fat version of Eton mess is the perfect dessert for a summer's evening, but be sure to limit yourself to just one portion.

Calories 127 kCals

Serves 4

400 g (13 oz) strawberries, washed and hulled, plus extra to decorate
1 tablespoon icing sugar
300 g (10 oz) low-fat fromage frais
4 ready-made meringue nests

1   Mash the strawberries with the icing sugar using a fork or food processor.

2   Put the fromage frais in a separate bowl, crumble in the meringues and mix together lightly.

3   Add the strawberry mixture and fold together with a spoon until marbled. Spoon into glasses, decorate with strawberry halves, and serve immediately.

TWISTS & VARIATIONS

Any combination of fresh berries works well here, including raspberries, blackberries, blueberries and even a handful of juicy blackcurrants.

Red pepper & spring onion dip

These dips are ideal served with vegetable batons or even mini wholemeal pitta breads or breadsticks. They taste so good you'll even be spreading them on toast!

Calories 83 kCals

Serves 4

1 large red pepper, cut into quarters, cored and deseeded
2 garlic cloves, unpeeled
250 g (8 oz) low-fat natural yogurt
2 spring onions, finely chopped
black pepper
selection of raw vegetables, cut into batons, to serve

1 Slightly flatten the pepper quarters and place on a baking sheet. Wrap the garlic in foil and place on the sheet. Roast in a preheated oven, 220°C (425°F), Gas Mark 7, for 30–40 minutes until the pepper is slightly charred and the garlic is soft.

2 When cool enough to handle, remove the skin from the pepper and discard. Cut the flesh into dice and transfer to a bowl. Squeeze the roasted garlic flesh from the cloves into the bowl.

3 Using a fork, roughly mash the pepper and garlic together. Stir in the yogurt and spring onions. Season to taste with black pepper and serve with the vegetable batons.

Hummus

Calories 264 kCals

Serves 4

1 x 425 g (14 oz) can chickpeas, drained and rinsed
juice of 1 lemon
1 garlic clove, sliced
1 tablespoon olive oil
pinch of cayenne pepper
100 g (3½ oz) tahini
salt and black pepper
selection of raw vegetables, cut into batons, to serve

To serve
1 teaspoon extra virgin olive oil
pinch of cayenne pepper
1 tablespoon flat leaf parsley

1 Put the chickpeas in a food processor or blender and whizz to a smooth purée. Add the lemon juice, garlic, olive oil, cayenne pepper and tahini and blend again until creamy.

2 Season with salt and black pepper and transfer to a serving dish. Drizzle with oil and sprinkle with cayenne pepper and parsley and serve with vegetable batons.

Your fitness programme

The Biggest Loser fitness programme is designed to incinerate calories and fat, leaving you toned, fit and super-healthy. It will fire up your metabolism as well as ratchet up your rate of weight loss. So, turn off the TV, sit up straight and get ready for action.

Introducing your new fitness programme

Pull up your socks and lace your trainers. We're going to put you through your paces to get that weight off once and for all. You'll be working harder than you've ever worked before, but you'll have the best reason of all for doing it – you!

Chances are that exercise hasn't been high on your list of priorities for a while. Excess weight is not just the result of overeating but also of under-exercising. Exercise burns fat and creates the muscle that burns even more. It hones, tightens and tones your physique, so you'll look fit and trim – and feel great. The benefits will start from the very first session.

Health benefits of exercise

- A lower risk of heart disease, stroke and many types of cancer
- Improved resistance to disease
- More efficient digestion
- Reduced blood pressure and cholesterol levels
- More stable blood-sugar levels, which can prevent cravings
- A faster metabolism
- More restful sleep
- Fewer mood swings and less anxiety and depression
- Less stress, as exercise soaks up the adrenaline created by stressful situations
- Reduced joint and muscle pain as you gain strength
- Stronger bones and reduced risk of osteoporosis
- Weight loss and maintenance
- Increased self-confidence and self-esteem
- Higher levels of energy and endurance

What's involved?

There are several different types of exercise but we're just going to focus on two.

We'll be pushing you through some tough cardio sessions (see pages 92–98), which will literally burn off calories and fat, and keep your metabolism pumping on overdrive. Alongside those, you'll be doing strength-training exercises (see pages 99–173), which are designed to build muscles all over your body, leaving you stronger, tighter and more toned than you've ever been before. Better still, the muscles you're creating will become fat-burning machines, that will keep your metabolic rate high and the excess pounds firmly off!

The six-week Biggest Loser exercise programme will give you a good balance of both cardio and strength training, but you're going to have to shuffle your daily schedule to fit it all in. No excuses; you can't shift weight without building muscle and burning calories. This is an essential part of becoming a Biggest Loser, so prepare yourself.

Think an hour of exercise a day is ridiculous? It's not. Being 63 kg (10 stone) overweight is ridiculous!

Cardio workouts

Cardiovascular exercise is sustained and rhythmic activity that involves working the large muscles in your body (such as those in your legs). Cardio makes your heart and lungs work harder to pump oxygen to the muscles to make them contract. It's also known as 'aerobic', which literally means 'with air'. If you're working hard enough during a cardio session, you should be sweating, as your body tries to cool itself down, and getting short of breath to the point where it is difficult to finish a sentence without taking a breath in the middle.

What is cardio exercise?
Think of cardio exercise as being long in duration, with low or medium intensity.

Cardio exercises
- Brisk walking
- Jogging
- Running
- Running up stairs
- Cycling
- Rowing
- Dancing
- Competitive football
- Tennis
- Swimming
- Skiing
- Kickboxing

If you are in the gym
- Elliptical trainer
- Rower, stairmaster
- Stationary bike
- Treadmill

Strength workouts

Strength training (also known as 'conditioning' or 'resistance training') basically uses muscle contractions – normally against some form of resistance, such as weights or even gravity – to build strength and endurance. As you lose weight, strength training will tone and firm the flabby bits and give you some attractive muscle definition. Don't worry, girls, you won't end up looking like an Olympic shot-putter with the kind of routines we're recommending.

Unless you keep on nuking those calories and your body fat with exercise, your weight loss will grind to a halt.

The Biggest Loser fitness programme focuses on all the key muscle groups, to ensure that your whole body achieves optimum fitness and performance. We don't believe that 'spot' training – for example, targeting your hips or thighs – has as much impact on your overall shape, size and weight as whole-body strength training will. Following our programme, you'll tighten up your legs, chest, back, core and arms without creating any imbalances.

To make the strength training part of your programme more effective, you'll be increasing the number of repetitions (reps) as the weeks pass, and decreasing the time you rest in between exercises. And if things seem to be getting too easy, you can increase the weight of your dumbbells as well. The idea behind strength training is to push your muscles to the max, until you feel them burn. That's how you'll know it's working.

YOUR FITNESS PROGRAMME

Benefits of strength training

- Improves overall health and wellbeing
- Increases bone density
- Improves muscle, tendon and ligament strength and flexibility
- Enhances joint function
- Reduces the risk of injury
- Temporarily increases metabolism
- Affects long-term metabolism by building muscle
- Improves heart function

Combining the two

At the outset of the programme, you'll aim for five 60-minute workouts a week, alternating cardio and strength training. As your fitness and endurance improve, you'll need to push yourself a little harder. This means adding in a couple of sessions every week until, by the end of Week 6, you'll be doing ten workouts every week – half cardio and half strengthening. Yes, that's more than one a day!

Look at it this way: if you can make it to the gym once or twice a week, perform a few strength-training workouts while watching telly in the evening, go for a run, and take an aerobics or salsa class, you're almost there. Get into the habit of exercising first thing in the morning, even if you can only fit in 30 minutes of cardio – cycling to work, for example, watching the morning news on your stationary cycle, going for an early-morning swim, or a run in the park. You'll feel so great, you'll be ready for more after work, too.

Exercise encourages your body to release hormones known as 'endorphins', which lift your mood, leaving you full of energy and determination. You'll soon get addicted to that exercise 'high' and you'll find you want to get back out there and push some more.

Excuses, excuses ...
We've heard them all, but the one that crops up most often is people saying they've no time for exercise. If this is you, jot down in your Biggest Loser notebook the amount of time you spend watching telly every day. Honestly. Then tot up the time you spend on social networking sites or chatting on the phone.

Most people have at least an hour they could spare after they finish work and many have several. Even if you're a single parent, once the kids are in bed you could get your dumbbells out and get down on a rug in the sitting room.

Get your priorities right. Either decide you're in this to win or that you'd rather sit on your butt getting fatter. Just make sure you're honest with yourself.

Caution

Are you fit to exercise? Run through the following checklist:

- Are you over 40?
- Is it more than a year since you last exercised?
- Are you aiming to lose more than a fifth of your current body weight?
- Do you suffer from any joint or bone problems?
- Do you ever get chest pains?
- Have you been diagnosed with a heart condition?
- Are you taking medication for high blood pressure?
- Have you ever got so dizzy that you've lost your balance?
- Do you have a chronic condition, such as asthma, that could affect your ability to exercise?
- Have you ever been told that you should exercise only under medical supervision?

If you answer 'yes' to any of these questions, you should see your doctor before starting the Biggest Loser programme. Don't think this is a get-out clause, though. You'll still be expected to work out, but there may be some precautions you need to take.

Understanding the basics

You may not be familiar with all the terms that will crop up in the exercise programme. Here's a quick explanation of the ones you'll need to bear in mind.

Sets We've arranged the exercises into sets so that you work all the key muscle groups in each workout, doing a certain number of reps (repetitions) according to your fitness level (beginner, intermediate or advanced – see page 174 for a guide to which level best suits you), and resting for a certain length of time in between. You'll increase the number of sets and reps and decrease your resting time between exercises as you get fitter.

Lactic acid Some types of exercise (such as strength training) require energy to be produced faster than our bodies can deliver oxygen. In this case, lactic acid is produced in the muscles, which causes a burning sensation. So when we talk about a lactic-acid burn, we mean the feeling you get when you push yourself to the max. You'll be doing a lot of this.

Neutral spine This is the natural position of the spine in which its three curves are retained: a small hollow at the base of the neck, a slight roundness in the mid-back and an arch in the lower back. A neutral spine is neither rounded forwards nor arched back too much. Your spine is strongest when it's in this position because it's naturally supported by your muscles. Don't try to force your back flat – keep those curves as you exercise.

Core stability Your 'core' is the set of muscles deep within your abdomen, which run the length of your body to connect to the spine and pelvis, and help to create good posture and enable movement. When your core is strong, you can exercise without overbalancing. Imagine throwing a cannonball from a canoe. The canoe would jerk backwards, wouldn't it? If you try to perform an exercise without a strong core, the same could happen to you – either that or you might strain your back. When you are asked in an exercise to 'stabilize', 'engage' or 'brace' your core, it simply means to pull in your navel and squeeze your butt so that your muscles are activated and ready to support you.

Muscles There are hundreds of muscles in the human body, all with their own particular functions, but the bigger ones tend to work in groups. In fact, very few muscles work in isolation. When you contract one set of muscles, another set on the opposite side of the body will be stretching. For example, when you straighten a bent leg you'll be contracting the quads and stretching the hamstrings. Fortunately, you don't need to learn the names of all these muscles (unless you're training as a medical professional). There are just a few that crop up time and again in the exercises (mainly those to do with legs, bums and tums!), and it's worth knowing where they are. Go through the diagram opposite and try to identify all the muscles listed in your own body. Can't find your rectus abdominus beneath the layer of blubber? Don't worry – you soon will. Try Angie's Dumbbell Russian Twist (see page 138) and you'll feel it, even if you can't see it!

Biceps
Bend your elbow and
clench your fist to see
these in the upper arms

Pectoralis major (pecs)
Just above your
boobs – or moobs

Deltoid
Over the curve of the shoulder

Trapezius
Hunch your
shoulders to feel this

Triceps
Backs of the
upper arms

Obliques
Round the sides
of your waist

ansverse abdominals
muscles used to pull
your navel in

Rhomboids
These squeeze
your shoulder blades
together

Rectus abdominis
rom the breastbone
to the pubic bone

Gluteus maximus (glutes)
The buttock muscles

Hamstrings
In the backs of the thighs

Quadriceps (quads)
At the fronts of
the thighs

Calves
Backs of your lower legs

Getting started

Once you've set your starting date, it's time to get yourself prepared. All the Biggest Loser exercises are designed so that you can do them at home with the minimum of equipment – so there are no excuses for not getting on with it.

What you'll need

Footwear You don't need fancy shoes to train. Choose comfortable, well-fitting trainers that support your feet but are light and flexible enough for any kind of exercise.

Exercise kit Wear light, comfortable clothing in layers, so you can peel it off or pile it on according to your body temperature.

Water Make sure you are well hydrated before exercise; performance suffers with even mild dehydration and you can end up feeling sick and dizzy. Drink a couple of glasses before exercise and another couple within 20 minutes of finishing.

Dumbbells Weights are used in most of the strength-training drills to enhance the effects. Don't go too low, or you won't challenge your muscles enough. Women can usually manage between 4 and 8 kg (8–16 lb); guys, go for something between 6 and 12 kg (12–24 lb). The moment it all seems easy, buy some heavier weights. Bottled water makes a great dumbbell; start at 1 litre (1¾ pints), increasing to 1.5 litres (2½ pints) then 2 litres (3½ pints).

Joining a gym?

You don't need to join a gym to do any of the drills in the Biggest Loser programme; however, you might find you benefit from the support of gym staff, the company of other Losers and a little variety. If you can vary your cardio sessions with gym equipment such as running or rowing machines, or sign up for some high-intensity exercise classes, it will keep things interesting. And once you've paid for gym membership you'll have an added incentive to turn up to get your money's worth.

Make a few lifestyle changes, too – walking the dog, playing with the kids in the park, cycling to work or getting off the bus one stop earlier will all benefit your new fitness regime.

Not sure whether your dumbbells are the right weight for you? If you can lift them, you can work out with them. Go as high as you comfortably can.

Motivate yourself!

Get your Biggest Loser notebook out and remind yourself of the reasons why you're doing this. Drag out your 'before' picture and take a good long look. Now envision yourself at the weight you want to be and make some appointments for exercise. Slot them into your diary just as you do social engagements and work commitments. Make a date with a buddy, so you'll have to go. Pay for classes in advance, so you'll lose money if you don't make it. Be aware that every reason why you can't exercise 'today' is just an excuse. Banish excuses from your life!

Finally …

No exercise session – cardio or strength training – should be undertaken without a 5- to 10-minute warm-up before and a cool-down after. We've got some good ones laid out in the programme (see pages 100–103 and 170–173). If you rush into exercise without warming those muscles, you're going to hurt yourself; and if you plonk in front of the telly afterwards without cooling down, you're just asking for trouble.

Are you ready now? Time to get fit!

Cardio exercise

Cardio burns calories and fat, gets your heart pumping, your blood full of oxygen and your endorphins flowing.

For the next 6 weeks – and beyond – you are going to be putting in at least an hour of cardio every other day, for five days a week. You're doing this to lose weight, and cardio increases your metabolic rate and literally burns fat. It's not a negotiable part of your Biggest Loser programme.

Getting things going
OK, you know that cardio is the type of exercise that moves your big muscles (those in your legs and arms, for example), and you know that it involves constant movement for at least 20 minutes, at a rate that makes you sweat and get out of breath.

There are lots of different kinds of cardio to choose from. It doesn't matter what you do; the important thing is that you do it for long enough. If you can't manage 60 minutes in one go, then break it down into 20- or 30-minute chunks. The important thing is that you have to do an hour of cardio on a cardio day. (These are set out in the Weekly Workout Guide on pages 182–183.)

Sprinting gets your heart rate up fast and pushes your whole body to the limit.

The best thing about cardio is that you can do it almost anywhere and squeeze it into even the busiest schedule. Try brisk walking to work instead of jumping on the bus, or leap on your exercise bike, or pick up a skipping rope when you've got the kids in bed – there's no reason why you can't exercise in front of the telly. Use the commercial breaks to run up and down the stairs and really get your heart rate up, then jog on the spot when your programme resumes. Hit the swimming pool or the tennis court in your lunch break, or sign yourself up for an aerobics class first thing every morning. As long as you are sweating, and getting your heart and lungs pumping, you are burning calories.

Your running technique
Running is one of the most effective fat-burning exercises but it can be hard on the knees if your technique is wrong. If you're not used to running, ask a personal trainer to watch you and give advice. People's running styles are very individual, so if you feel pain or strain as you pound the pavements, it could be that it's not the exercise for you.

Jogging is fantastic aerobic exercise; find your pace and sustain it for at least 30 minutes.

Starting cardio slowly

If you want a fantastic body, you've got to want it more than you want to sit on your butt and eat rubbish.

If fitness has been low on your list of priorities, start cardio exercises gently. That doesn't mean shorter sessions, but working your way up in terms of intensity. At first, it might be hard to sustain even a gentle jog for your target 60 minutes, so start by running for a few minutes, walking, running, walking and so on. In as little as a couple of weeks, you'll be running more than you are walking. By six weeks, we expect you to be able to manage at least 20 minutes in one go.

It's got to hurt to work, so don't give up at the first hurdle. Push yourself as hard as you can, and even when you have to reduce the intensity a bit, keep on moving. Don't sit down and rest; the point of cardio is to keep your heart pumping at the same rate. Drink plenty of water, listen to some great music and really push yourself.

How do you know when your body is working at the right level? If you can feel your heart pumping, if you are breathing heavily but still able to talk, and if you are, most importantly, sweating, you've got it right. Carry on at the same intensity and pace until your session is finished, and you'll be creating the optimum environment for major weight loss.

Squats burn calories and tone your butt and thighs at the same time.

A social activity

This may be news to you, but cardio exercise, such as power walking or jogging, can be a social activity, giving you the perfect opportunity to catch up with friends who are also trying to shed those pounds. Exercising with somebody else – or even your dog – can help keep you motivated too, as you spur each other on to go the extra mile even though you thought you could go no further.

Run to rhythm

Why not create your own personal playlist including all your favourite up-tempo tracks to motivate you during your cardio sessions? Listening to music that matches your stride while you're power walking or jogging will put a bounce in your step, boost your energy levels and help you to maintain a steady pace. And if you don't have time to pull together your own collection of tunes, there are plenty of compilations on the market that will do the job just as well.

Work up a sweat

Don't be afraid to work up a sweat during your cardio sessions. A good workout – one that causes sweat to drip down your face and back – is great news as it helps the body to eliminate harmful toxins, cleans out the skin's pores and helps regulate your temperature. What's more, when you sweat as a result of exercise, you also release hormones that make you feel good and act as a natural antidepressant.

Side jacks get your heart pumping and are ideal for squeezing in a little cardio.

Calories burned by cardio

Below you'll find the average calories burned for each hour of exercise for people of different weights.

ACTIVITY	YOUR WEIGHT				
	76 KG 12 STONE	89 KG 14 STONE	102 KG 16 STONE	127 KG 20 STONE	152 KG 24 STONE
BRISK WALKING	381 kCal	445 kCal	508 kCal	635 kCal	762 kCal
JOGGING	533 kCal	622 kCal	711 kCal	889 kCal	1,067 kCal
RUNNING	876 kCal	1,022 kCal	1,372 kCal	1,715 kCal	2,057 kCal
RUNNING UP STAIRS	1,143 kCal	1,334 kCal	1,524 kCal	1,905 kCal	2,286 kCal
CYCLING	610 kCal	711 kCal	813 kCal	1,016 kCal	1,219 kCal
ROWING	914 kCal	1,067 kCal	1,219 kCal	1,524 kCal	1,829 kCal
DANCING	495 kCal	578 kCal	660 kCal	826 kCal	991 kCal
FOOTBALL (COMPETITIVE)	762 kCal	889 kCal	1,016 kCal	1,143 kCal	1,372 kCal
TENNIS	533 kCal	622 kCal	711 kCal	889 kCal	1,067 kCal
SWIMMING	533 kCal	622 kCal	711 kCal	889 kCal	1,067 kCal
SKIING	533 kCal	622 kCal	711 kCal	889 kCal	1,067 kCal
KICKBOXING	762 kCal	889 kCal	1,016 kCal	1,270 kCal	1,524 kCal

The whole Biggest Loser ethos is to burn more calories than you eat – forcing your body to rely on fat stores for energy. Every calorie you incinerate means accelerated weight-loss – and that's what you're after.

If you are starting out obese, you have one big advantage over your skinnier pals – you'll burn more calories than them when doing exactly the same amount of exercise. As you'll see from the chart opposite, someone weighing 76 kg (12 stone) who runs for an hour will burn 876 calories, while someone of twice that weight will burn 2,057 calories – more than twice as many. It's just about the only benefit of being obese, so celebrate it!

If you slip up during your programme and scoff three Mars ® bars on the trot, you can do some extra cardio to compensate. A 58 g (2¼ oz) Mars ® bar has approximately 260 calories, so three have 780. Look down the column for your weight to see what you'll have to do to shed those excess calories. Although you don't count calories on the Biggest Loser plan, it's worth being aware just how long it would take you to burn off those naughty snacks. Find out the calorie counts for the ones that tempt you and think about whether you really want them if you have to run up stairs for an hour afterwards.

Step aerobics is a great high-intensity cardio exercise.

THE EXERCISES

THIS COMPREHENSIVE COLLECTION of Biggest Loser exercises has been specially devised by our trainers to help you burn calories, build fat-burning muscle mass, and tone and strengthen your body. The exercises are divided by body part (legs, chest, back, core, arms, and multijoint complexes) and, if performed regularly, will help you to achieve your weight-loss goal.

Warm-up exercises

THE WARM-UP ISN'T OPTIONAL. It will take a good 10 minutes to get your blood flowing, your muscles and joints loosened up, and your spine mobile and aligned, ready for an exercise session.

Head turn

Stand straight, shoulders back, with heels, knees, hips and shoulders in line. Place one hand on your head. Bend your right ear towards your right shoulder. Straighten up and repeat on the left. Straighten up and bend your chin to your chest. Tip your head back as far as you can. Repeat 8 times.

Shoulder roll

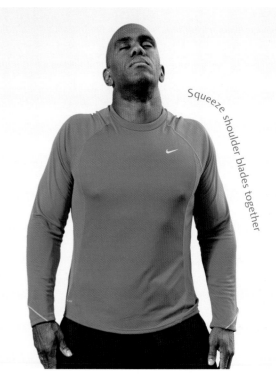

Squeeze shoulder blades together

Hunch your shoulders up towards your ears and then let them drop down again. Roll them forwards 5 or 6 times then backwards 5 or 6 times, squeezing your shoulder blades together on the backwards roll. Keep your arms hanging loose and relaxed throughout.

Hip rotation

1 Stand comfortably, with your feet
shoulder-width apart, knees slightly
bent and your spine neutral. Place
your hands on your hips and look
straight ahead.

2 Brace your core muscles and
draw a slow circle with your pelvis,
moving it clockwise (to the right) in
a circle. Push to the right, back, to
the left and then out in front. Repeat
10 times.

3 Now circle your pelvis in
the opposite direction
(anti-clockwise), really pushing your
hips as far as you can to make a big
circle. Once again, do 10 repetitions.

TOP TIP

If you spend lots
of time sitting
down, do plenty
of rotations to
get rid of stiffness
in your hips.

Backstroke

This is a dynamic warm-up for your whole upper body. Keep your core braced throughout.

Stand with your feet shoulder-width apart and knees slightly bent. Brace your core muscles then reach up and back with your left arm, opening up your shoulder girdle. As your left arm comes down the back, raise your right arm and bring it up and over in a fluid movement. Do 20 repetitions with each arm.

Brace your core muscles

Front crawl

Now you are going to go the other way, to continue opening up your chest and shoulders. Get a good rhythm going as you circle around, using the same movement as you would in a swimming pool.

Brace your core muscles and raise your right arm then push it down in front of you and then behind you. As the right arm comes up and over, bring your left arm back and circle 20 times with each arm.

Bow

The Bow mobilizes and warms up the lower back, stretching your hamstrings and toning your glutes.

1 Stand with a neutral spine and place your hands on your lower back, one on top of the other.

2 Lean forwards in a bow from the hip, keeping your spine neutral, shoulders back, core braced and chin up. Squeeze your glutes to make sure your hips stay straight. Hold for a few seconds then straighten up. Repeat for around 2 minutes.

Overhead bow

This is a big, dynamic movement that will get your whole body fired and will open up your torso, arms and hips.

1 Standing with your feet flat on the floor and your legs wide apart, raise your arms up above your head. Really stretch them up, until you feel your chest and back opening.

2 Come down in a deep squat and reach your hands through your legs and behind your ankles as far as you can go. The key is to drop really low, getting your butt down, so that you feel a stretch right through your hips and thighs. Stand up again and repeat 20 times.

Leg exercises

TRAINING THE LEGS will make your cardio work
more efficient and will also improve your posture.
Key muscles include your gluteals or 'glutes'
(the muscles covering your butt); quadriceps
or 'quads' (in the fronts of your thighs);
and hamstrings (at the backs of
the thighs).

Bodyweight squat

This is a great drill for the whole leg. Your ultimate goal is a 90-degree angle at the hips, but it can take some time to reach this. Push yourself right to the edge.

Head facing forwards

90-degree angle at hips

2 Now drop down by bending your knees and pulling back your hips, keeping your head up and your shoulders back. Bring your arms forwards for balance. Stop at the bottom of your squat, so you can re-brace your core. Now, put your palms together and squeeze your glutes to drive up to standing position again.

1 Stand straight, with a neutral spine, shoulders back, head up, arms by your sides and core engaged. You'll be actively using your core muscles in the squat.

Dumbbell squat

Dumbbells up the impact of this drill, which works the quads, glutes, hamstrings and hips. Keep your dumbbell close to your body, so it doesn't pull you over.

Weight close to your body

Hips back

TOP TIP

Breathe in into a dynamic, powerful squat, and exhale as you drive up again.

1 Stand with your legs shoulder-width apart and your head up, looking forwards. Hold a dumbbell between your hands, in front of your upper chest. You'll be making the same movement as in the Bodyweight Squats (see page 105).

2 Take a breath in, bend your knees, pull your hips back and drop down. Keep your arms – and your dumbbell – in the same position in front of your chest. Stop at the bottom of your squat then drive up again, breathing out.

Plyometric squat

'Plyometric' means the exercise has a 'bounce' in it. These star-jumps give all the benefits of a traditional squat but with a high-intensity twist that burns calories.

1 Stand with your feet shoulder-width apart, eyes looking straight ahead. Bend your arms forwards to get some momentum, and bend your knees slightly.

2 Pull back your hips, bend your knees and drop down into a squat – as low as you can go. Swing your arms back and when you get to the bottom, take a second to brace your core.

3 Now JUMP as high as you can, with your arms and legs outstretched in a star shape. As you come down, draw in your legs and arms. On landing, push straight down into your squat again. Keep the movement fluid and dynamic, going as fast as you can, while maintaining your core.

Deadlift

This is a fantastic drill for building fat-burning muscle mass in your legs, and strengthening all the major muscle groups of your back and core.

Shoulders back

Neutral spine

1 Stand with your feet a little wider than shoulder-width apart, shoulders back. Hold a dumbbell between both hands in front of your groin.

2 Get into the deadlift position by bowing forwards, using your hips, hamstrings and glutes to drive your hips back, and squeezing your butt when you finish. Stop when you feel a stretch in your hamstrings. Your arms will drop so the weight hangs between your lower legs. Keep your eyes on the horizon.

3 Drive your hips forwards, using the same muscles to push yourself back up to standing position. Keep a neutral spine throughout. Continue the movement: drive hips back, push down, drive hips forwards, push up.

Single-leg deadlift

These can be challenging, so take your time until you get them right. They'll give your hamstrings a stretch and work all of your leg muscles simultaneously.

2 Bow forwards, and let the dumbbell slowly pull you down. Your right leg will naturally raise behind you. Lean forwards, keeping your chin up and a neutral spine, until you feel a stretch in your hamstring. Stop there, and drive through the hip, squeezing your glutes, to push back up again.

Chin up

Squeeze your glutes

1 Stand on your left leg, shoulders back, with your dumbbell held at thigh-level in front of your left leg. All of your weight is on one leg, so take time to stabilize.

Static lunge

This is a simple but effective drill for the legs, working the glutes and hamstrings on the front leg and the quads and calves on the back.

Feet facing forwards

90-degree angle (knee)

1 Stand straight and take a big step forwards, planting your left foot on the floor in front of you, and making sure that both feet are facing front. Keep your shoulders back and arms hanging loosely by your sides.

2 Bend your right knee towards the floor so that your hips drop down until there is a 90-degree angle at your left hip. Pause, then drive up through the left leg to raise yourself slowly. Alternate legs with each repetition.

ALTERNATIVE EXERCISE

Try this with a weight in each hand, palms facing inwards and elbows slightly bent, to increase the amount of work done and maximize the effects.

Moving lunge

This version of the lunge should be a flowing, continuous movement. Push yourself until you feel your hamstrings stretched, then drive yourself up as quickly as you can.

1 Stand straight with your arms by your sides. Brace your core and make sure your spine is neutral.

Brace your core

Land gently

2 Stride forwards with your left leg and go straight down into a lunge in the same movement. Don't crash in with your knee; land gently, as if you are stepping on to a sheet of ice that you don't want to break. It can be tricky the first few times, so stop at the bottom of the lunge and check that you've got your position right. Is your spine still in alignment?

3 Re-brace your core, then drive back up as powerfully as you can through your front leg. Get a good tempo going as you lunge and drive up. Once you've mastered the movement, try it while holding weights (see opposite).

Bulgarian split squat

This is a tough drill that will max out your hamstrings, glutes and quads. Get the correct position, with your foot firmly on a chair or low table for support.

Arms slightly bent

Foot facing forwards

1 Stand about one pace in front of a low table or chair. Rest the toes of your right foot on the surface. Keep your left foot pointing forwards. Hold the weights firmly by your sides, with arms slightly bent, palms facing inwards.

2 Slowly bend your left knee, keeping a straight posture, aiming to hit a 90-degree angle at the knee. At the bottom of the squat, stop and drive up through your left leg. Don't just drop – it's a slow, active pull-down, a stop, and then a powerful drive up.

90-degree angle (knee)

Isometric squat

Isometric exercises involve holding a position in order to strengthen the muscles. Even though you are not moving, you will feel a burn in your thighs and butt.

Head up

Arms at shoulder height

Neutral spine

1 Get yourself into a normal squat position (see page 105), with your arms held forwards at shoulder height. Your spine should be neutral, your head up, and your feet straight – heels behind toes. Now hold the squat for as long as possible – at least 30 seconds, more if you can.

TOP TIP

If it's burning, it's working, so hold that squat for as long as you can.

Dumbbell squat kick

This drill is a lot more cardiovascular than a traditional squat, so you'll be burning calories and making muscle. Alternate the leg you kick with as you do the repetitions.

1 Stand holding your dumbbells by your sides, palms facing inwards, arms relaxed, spine neutral and chin up. Your feet should be about shoulder-width apart, facing forwards.

2 Squat, driving your hips back and maintaining a neutral spine. Keep your knees behind your toes. Hold your position and make sure your core is stable.

3 Once you've reached the bottom of your squat, push your hips forwards, rise and kick out to the front, lifting your foot as high as you can. Drop down into your squat again.

ALTERNATIVE EXERCISE

If you can't manage to go from a squat to a high kick, do a lower kick instead. Whatever you do, don't compromise your squat position by letting your knees stick out beyond your toes, which will put you off balance.

Frog squat

Done correctly, this exercise works your thighs and glutes. Really small bounces will have maximum impact – but give it a miss if you've got knee problems.

Deep squat

Bounce in the air

1 Squat down like a frog, knees bent and wide apart, with your fingers splayed and fingertips just touching the ground between your feet.

2 Bounce about 10 cm (4 inches) into the air, using your thighs to create the movement. Do about 15 or 20 small bounces as fast as you can and you should feel a burn in your thighs.

Single-leg plyometric hop

This drill gets your heart pumping. Don't jump too high – even small jumps or bounces will target your glutes, hamstrings and thighs.

Arms at eye level

Land softly

1 Stand on your right leg, with the knee slightly bent, and push your left foot as far back as you can. Arms should be relaxed. Find a spot on the floor a couple of metres in front of you and fix your eyes on it.

2 Now, jump up on your right leg, raising your arms to eye level to increase the momentum.

3 Land softly on your left leg, bending your knee to absorb your weight. Keep your chin up. Hop from leg to leg as you repeat the movement.

Top tips for cardio exercises

1 **WALKING AND JOGGING**
Walking should be brisk. A stroll with your dog will not cut it unless he's a greyhound in a park full of squirrels. Jogging should be faster than walking, and close to a run.

FOOTBALL AND TENNIS
If you are standing on the sidelines waiting around for the ball, you're not doing cardio. It's ball chasing we're after here.

2 **SWIMMING**
Slow, gentle breaststroke may relax you, but is unlikely to raise your heart rate. Push yourself until you are out of breath. If you are not a confident swimmer, take lessons to perfect your technique.

5 **CYCLING**
If you can feel a gentle breeze on your face, pump a little harder. Choose a route with some hills in it.

3 **SKIPPING**
The temptation is to bash it out, but slower, rhythmic skipping lasting for at least 20 minutes will have more of an impact.

6 **DANCING**
Go for full-on disco, salsa, street or serious ballroom. Shimmying and gliding will not burn fat.

Sideways step-up

This is great for toning quads and glutes. Carry on until you are breaking a sweat. You can use the bottom step of your stairs or any object that will take your weight.

1 Stand alongside your step, place your right foot in the middle of it and press your palms together in front of your abdomen.

2 Quickly bring up your left foot, touch it on the step beside your right foot, then bring it back down again. This is a sideways motion; don't step forwards. Keep repeating until you're sweating and your muscles are burning, then turn round and swap legs.

ALTERNATIVE EXERCISE

To make this drill harder, when you step up, bring your knee to your chest before stepping down again. The higher the knee, the more effective the exercise will be.

Chest exercises

YOUR CHEST MUSCLES are known as your *pectoralis* ('pecs' for short), and they cover your entire upper ribcage. They're so big that you need a range of different exercises to target the various parts.

Bodyweight press-up

Press-ups are the ultimate exercise for the pecs. Drive up through your core and your chest at the same time, keeping a neutral spine. Don't dip at the hip.

1 Place your hands flat on the floor beneath your shoulders, with your elbows tucked in to your sides and toes curled under. Push yourself up into the 'plank position', keeping a straight back and a locked core and resting your weight on your hands and toes. Keep your body rigid.

2 Now press up, straightening your arms, driving up through your core and chest at the same time. Once your arms are straight, keep your abs engaged and bend your elbows to lower yourself back down. If you're struggling, start by pushing up from your knees until you get stronger.

No dip at the hips

Abs engaged

Arms straight

TOP TIP

Everyone should be able to do press-ups. Keep working at it.

Rotational push-up

This not only works your pecs, triceps and shoulders, but the rotation works your core muscles, too, so it's a great all-rounder to get your upper body trim.

palm outstretched

2 Lift your left arm so you're balancing your weight on your right hand, then swing up and really stretch the left arm above you. Swing it back down, then lower yourself to the ground. On your next press-up, lift your right arm up, balancing on your left. Keep alternating arms with each repetition.

1 Get yourself into the Bodyweight Press-up position (see page 119), hands beneath your shoulders, toes on the floor, back aligned. Now press up until your arms are straight.

Balance weight on hand

TOP TIP

Get a swinging rhythm going: Push up, swing your arm up, swing your arm down, push down.

Plyometric dumbbell chest press into crunch

This is a high-intensity drill in which you push up into a crunch. It's a bit like doing a bench press, but here you're lifting your upper body right off the ground.

1 Lie on your back, knees bent, feet on the floor. Rest your elbows on the floor at shoulder level, with your weights held directly above them.

2 Push the dumbbells up into the air until your arms are straight but don't lock your elbows.

3 As part of the same movement, lift your upper body and punch towards the ceiling. When you reach the top of the crunch, stop and reverse down again. Get a good momentum going: arms up, crunch, unroll, arms down. Breathe out with the exertion and breathe in as you roll down.

Punch towards ceiling

90-degree angle (knees)

Upper body off floor

Dumbbell fly

This will strengthen your pecs, which can lift a woman's bust and help eradicate man boobs, but it will take some perseverance to get it right.

Feet hip-width apart

1 Lie on your back with your knees bent and feet hip-width apart. Hold a dumbbell in each hand and press them together, arms very slightly bent, above your breast bone.

Chin up

2 Lower the dumbbells by opening your arms outwards, keeping the same slight bend at the elbow. Stop when your elbows reach the floor. Breathe out and drive up through the chest and the core at the same time to get back to the starting position.

Elbows slightly bent

Dumbbell fly single arm

Do more repetitions on your weaker side to create symmetry. If you can't feel a pull on your pecs, increase the weights by a kilogram or two (2–4 lb).

1 Get into the starting position for the Dumbbell Fly (see opposite), with your feet flat on the floor and arms slightly bent at the elbow.

2 Take your left arm out to the side until your elbow hits the ground, keeping your right arm still. Keep both dumbbells in line with your breast bone.

3 Bring your left arm back up and take your right arm out to the side, in a fluid movement. So it's together, left arm down, up, together, right arm down, and so on.

Plyometric push-up

This builds explosive power and revs up your metabolic rate. Sprinters often use plyometric techniques, so get going on this one if you want the body of an athlete.

1 Get yourself in the starting position for the Bodyweight Press-up (see page 119), with your hands slightly wider than shoulder-width apart, resting your bodyweight on your toes and hands.

2 Jump up from your hands, just as high as you can, pushing yourself straight up in the air while keeping your legs and body aligned.

3 Land on your palms, with your elbows by your sides, and lower yourself down. Then start again.

ALTERNATIVE EXERCISE

If you find this too hard, start with your weight on your knees rather than on your toes. When you push up, clap your hands together at the height of your jump.

Diamond push-up

This gets your pecs working and also tightens your triceps, giving balance to your upper body. It's harder than it looks, but push yourself until you can't do any more.

1 Kneel on a mat with your feet crossed at the ankles. Make a diamond shape with your index fingers and thumbs on the mat in front of you. Rest your weight on your knees and hands, with your arms straight and elbows unlocked.

2 Lower yourself to the ground, keeping your elbows tightly by your sides, until your chin touches the floor. Pause, make sure your body is aligned, then press up again.

Dumbbell chest press

This is a little like a bench press, working your pecs, biceps and triceps. Breathe out as you lift, to drive with more power, and inhale when you get to the top.

1 Lie on your back on the floor with your knees bent, feet hip-width apart. Rest your upper arms on the floor at shoulder height and hold your weights directly above your elbows, palms facing forwards.

2 Brace your core and drive your arms straight up in front of you, until the weights meet each other at the top. Pause for a second, and then control the descent back to your starting position.

ALTERNATIVE EXERCISE

Alternate your arms – right arm up, and then left – getting a rhythm going and making your core work a little harder to keep the momentum. Breathe in at the top and release the breath in sharp puffs to keep the pressure in your core muscles on exertion.

Dumbbell close-grip chest press

This drill is only slightly different from the Dumbbell Chest Press, but it's working a whole new part of your chest – and giving your triceps an additional boost as well.

1 Lie on your back with your knees bent and feet flat on the floor. Rest your upper arms by your sides and hold the weights directly above your elbows, palms facing inwards.

Weights above shoulders

Elbows tucked in

TOP TIP

Lost your motivation? Give yourself a wake-up call with a good look at your 'before' picture.

2 Drive your arms up until they are straight and the weights are above your shoulders. Keep your elbows tucked in as you lower to the floor again.

Back exercises

JUST LIKE YOUR CHEST, your back is made up of
big muscle groups that can handle heavy weights.
They include the *latissimus dorsi* or 'lats' (on either
side of the back), the *rhomboids* (across your
shoulders) and the *trapezius* (a diamond-shaped
muscle stretching across the top of the back).

Dumbbell row

You'll work your lats and *rhomboids* with this rowing drill, as well as using isometric strength in your legs. It's a good all-rounder, if a little demanding!

Elbows close to body

90-degree angle (elbows)

Core engaged

1 Stand with your feet slightly wider than shoulder-width apart. Bend your knees and take a bow forwards to get into the correct position, letting the weights drop between your legs. Keep your spine neutral, shoulders back and eyes looking straight ahead.

2 With your core firmly engaged, use your back muscles to pull the weights up to your waist in a rowing motion. Breathe out as you lift and breathe in at the top. Pause for a second at the top and then slowly lower the weights again, keeping your elbows close to your body.

Lower back raise

A strong back is essential for good posture and breathing, as well as for preventing injury. Perfecting this exercise will help you to perform the others more easily.

1 Lie on your front, with your upper arms extending out at shoulder height and your elbows bent so that your forearms rest on the floor alongside your head. Rest your toes on the floor.

2 Lift your upper body from the waist, keeping your back and arms in line. Hold for about 2 seconds, lower for 2, and then repeat.

Back and arms in line

Toes on the floor

Bend from the waist

One-armed row

This exercise targets those muscles that you use when lifting and carrying – your lats, shoulders and triceps. Do as many drills as you can manage.

2 Pull up your dumbbell, driving through your elbow until you reach waist height. Keep looking straight ahead, and make sure your spine stays neutral. Lower to the starting position again. Complete the repetitions on one side then change position so your right knee is on the table or chair, and the weight is in your left hand.

1 Rest your left knee on a table or chair that's about knee-height. Place your left hand flat on the table or chair beneath your shoulder. Hold a dumbbell in your right hand, palm facing inwards. Your right knee should be close to the table or chair, right foot facing forwards.

Core exercises

CORE CONDITIONING will give you a flat, toned torso and a stable spine and pelvis, which provides a solid foundation for movement. Along with your 'abs' (*rectus abdominis*), core muscles include the obliques (which run around the sides of your abdomen), transverse abdominals (which are under the obliques), hip flexors and adductors, and your glutes.

Plank

This position engages and activates your core. Once it's mastered, the drills in this book will become easier and more effective – and your stomach will be flatter!

No dip at the hips

Elbows beneath shoulders

1 This is like the plank position you adopt as the starting position for a press-up (see page 119) but instead of resting your weight on your hands, you rest it on your forearms. Elbows should be directly beneath your shoulders, palms flat on the floor and your spine neutral. Look down at the floor. Don't let your hips drop beneath shoulder height. Squeeze your abs and hold for as long as you can until you feel a little shaky.

ALTERNATIVE EXERCISE

Make your body work harder by lifting one leg off the ground, while maintaining the same position. Hold for as long as you can, then repeat with the other leg.

Dumbbell crunch

The movement in this crunch should come from you contracting your abs to drive the dumbbell forwards. If you feel any strain in your neck, you're doing it wrong!

2 Contract your core further and crunch forwards, holding your weight in the same position. Your eyes will naturally look forwards over the tops of your knees. Pause and hold at the top, then slowly descend.

1 Lie on your back with your knees bent, feet fairly close to your butt, about hip-width apart. Grip a dumbbell with both hands just above your chest. It will remain in this position throughout. Engage your abs and use that movement to raise your head off the floor, without straining your neck.

Eyes on your weight

Lower back on ground

ALTERNATIVE EXERCISE
To make this exercise harder, take the weight up behind your head with your arms straight but not locked. Contract your abdominals to crunch upwards as before, bringing the dumbbell over towards your knees, then reverse back down again.

Triple crunch

Try to get a rhythm going here to work your abs to best effect. Remember: the movement should come from your core muscles, not your neck.

90-degree angle (hips)

Core engaged

Feet together

1 Lie on your back with your feet flat on the floor, about hip-width apart. Hold your dumbbell with both hands above your chest. Engage your core and use this contraction to raise your head slightly off the floor.

2 Contract your abs further and crunch up. Push your dumbbell straight up above your chest, and hold it there. Pause for a second, keeping your abs tight and your feet on the floor.

3 Crunch even further and hold your position, then slowly descend and lower the weight back down to just above your chest.

Reverse crunch

This is a great one for hitting that little pouch of fat that sits on your lower belly. It tightens your abs and turns them into fat-burning machines.

TOP TIP

If you aren't sweating, it's not working, so get yourself moving till you drip.

2 Using your hands for support, contract your abs and push up, lifting your hips off the floor. Push towards the ceiling, keeping your legs straight. Hold, and then descend slowly to the starting position.

1 Lie on your back, with your knees bent and arms by your sides, palms facing down. Engage your core, check your spine is neutral and lift your legs at right angles to your body.

Superman crunch

This is the best way to get the six-pack of a superhero, hence the name! Be sure always to lead with your chest, rather than with your head.

1 Lie on your back, knees bent and feet flat on the floor about hip-width apart. Hold two full bottles of water in the air above your shoulders, your palms facing forwards and your arms straight but not locked.

2 Engage your abs and crunch up, lifting your chest and head, while keeping your arms straight. It's much like the motion of a sit-up, but your arms remain in the air and you keep looking forwards. Hold your position for a few seconds, then slowly descend until your head is on the floor.

Arms straight

Knees bent

Dumbbell Russian twist

A great drill for your obliques – the 'love-handle' area on the sides of your waist. Focus on your core, making sure you get enough of a twist to tone those muscles.

2 Twist your upper body to the right, driving the dumbbell down towards the floor. Without allowing it to touch the floor, use your abs to reverse the twist and bring the dumbbell back up again.

1 Sit up straight and lean back on your butt, lifting your feet off the ground. The moment your legs rise, your core will be engaged. Take a second to find your balance. Hold a dumbbell steady in two hands, just above your abdomen.

3 Drive the dumbbell to the other side and down, then draw it back up. It's almost like the motion involved in paddling a kayak. Use your abs to keep you steady. If you are finding it tough, you can put your feet down on the floor until you get stronger.

Core engaged
Twist at the waist

Dumbbell side bend

This exercise strengthens and tightens your core muscles. Make sure that you keep looking straight ahead to maintain your posture.

1 Standing with your feet hip-width apart, hold a dumbbell in your right hand and raise the left to your forehead in a sailor salute. Your left upper arm should be at shoulder height, with fingertips touching the side of your brow, palm facing forwards.

Look straight ahead

Feet hip-width apart

2 Keeping your back straight and looking straight ahead, bend from the hip towards the right, stretching down towards the floor. Your left elbow will automatically point up towards the ceiling. Slowly draw yourself back up, switch the dumbbell to your other hand and repeat on the other side.

Abdominal twist

This is an effective drill to work your obliques, reduce your love handles and give a tight, toned look to your torso.

1 Lie on your back, your arms outstretched at shoulder height and palms facing up. Bend your legs and lift them so that they form a 90-degree angle at hips and knees. Place a bottle of water between your knees.

2 With your knees directly above your hips, and your bottle held firmly between them, roll your lower back and hips so that your knees rotate to the right. Keep your shoulders and arms pressed down on the floor.

Palms face upward

3 Use your abdominal muscles to bring your knees back up to the centre then twist to the left, still keeping your upper body firmly on the floor. Move slowly to one side then to the other, feeling the stretch in your lower back but making your abdominal muscles do the work.

Shoulders and arms stay on floor

Twisting windmill

This is a killer exercise for the uninitiated, but it's quality, not quantity that matters here. Take your time and you'll get a strong, balanced core and super-toned abs.

1 Lie flat on your back, with your arms outstretched at shoulder height and palms facing upwards. Engage your abs and lift your legs straight up in the air, keeping your feet together and your shoulders on the ground.

2 Roll your hips so that your legs rotate to the left, pushing as far as you can while keeping your shoulders and arms pressed to the floor.

3 Use your abdominals to bring your legs back up to centre, then roll them to your right. Stop if you feel any strain in your lower back, because that means your abs aren't yet strong enough to control the movement.

Legs straight in the air

90-degree angle (hips)

Abs engaged

Arm exercises

THERE'S NOTHING MORE ATTRACTIVE than firm, toned arms, with good muscle definition and the power you need to work out effectively. Key muscles are the biceps (at the front of the upper arm), the triceps (at the back of the upper arm) and the deltoids (which form the rounded contour of your shoulder).

21 bicep curls

This is what we call matrix training – evening out the whole range of muscles, and working each section until your whole arm is toned.

1 Stand with your shoulders back, chest out, legs straight, knees very slightly bent, feet pointing straight ahead and spine neutral. Hold your weights in each hand, palms facing up, at about hip level, with your arms straight but not locked.

2 Bend your elbows to lift the weights halfway up – to just below chest height. Do 7 curls up and down to this halfway point. Keep looking straight ahead and don't move anything other than your arms.

3 Now do 7 curls from the halfway point to just above shoulder level. Keep your elbows tucked in to your sides and use the muscles of your arms, not your shoulders. Finally, do 7 curls all the way from bottom to top, starting with your arms by your sides and finishing with the weights just above shoulder height. That's your 21!

Weights just above shoulder

Elbows tucked in

Dumbbell single standing press

This drill is great for your arms and shoulders. The key to success is to keep your core braced. If you don't, you'll injure your lower back.

Weight just above shoulder

2 Breathe out, brace your core and drive the dumbbell straight up overhead. Stop at the top so that you can control the deceleration back to your starting position. Pause at the bottom, re-brace and drive again.

Chin up

Core braced

1 Stand up straight, feet shoulder-width apart. Bend your knees slightly and brace your core. Hold a weight in your right hand, palm facing forwards, with your elbow bent out to the side so the weight is just above shoulder height. Keep your shoulders back to open up your chest.

Dumbbell double standing press

This works both sides of your body simultaneously. Make sure you breathe out on the up movement and in on the down.

Weights above shoulders

Arms straight

2 Push both arms up together, until they are straight and you feel your abs stretching. Hold the position for a few seconds, then slowly return to your starting position.

1 Stand with your feet directly beneath your shoulders and your back straight. Hold your weights in both hands, palms facing inwards, just above your shoulders. Look straight ahead and keep your neck strong.

Feet shoulder-width apart

Dumbbell lateral raise

This drill isn't easy, but if you keep your arms slightly bent and your shoulders back you'll be working the correct muscles, which will make it more achievable.

Weights by your sides

Arms at shoulder height

Slightly bent elbows

1 Stand straight with your feet beneath your shoulders and your knees very slightly bent. Engage your core and roll your shoulders back so that your spine is aligned. Getting your posture right will protect your neck. Hold your weights in each hand at hip height, palms facing inwards and elbows slightly bent.

2 Raise your dumbbells out to the sides until they are above shoulder height. Don't let your shoulders lift. Keep that slight bend in your arms. Your weights should stay in line with your body – not in front or behind it. Pause at the top, engage your core, and bring your weights down to the starting position again.

Anterior shoulder raise

This is a deceptively straightforward drill that will really push your arm and shoulder muscles, toning, tightening and creating plenty of fat-burning muscle.

Shoulders do the work

Knees slightly bent

Feet hip-width apart

Abs engaged

1 Stand with your feet hip-width apart and knees very slightly bent. Hold your weights by your sides with your palms facing backwards and your elbows slightly bent.

2 Engage your abs and lift your arms in front of you until the weights are in line with your shoulders with the palms facing down. Let your shoulders do all the work.

3 Raise your weights again, so that your arms are fully extended above your head and the weights are directly above your shoulders. Keep that slight bend in the elbows. Pause, re-engage your core, and bring the weights down to the starting position.

Dumbbell push press

This is the kind of technique you see weightlifters use in the Olympics, getting the power of their whole body to help drive the weights upwards.

Weights at shoulder height

Hips back

Knees bent

1 Stand with your legs hip-width apart, knees very slightly bent, shoulders back and weights held just above shoulder height, with your palms facing inwards.

2 Do a little dip by bending your knees and pushing back your hips, still keeping the dumbbells in the same position above shoulder height.

3 Push your arms up in an explosive drive, working from your core, until your arms are straight with the weights directly above your shoulders. Hold for a moment, re-engage your core, and then make a slow descent to the starting position.

Dumbbell upright row

This is a great drill for working the fronts of your shoulders, stabilizing your core and improving your posture. Keep your shoulders back, chin up and eyes forwards.

2 Draw the weights up towards your chin, bending your elbows outwards in a 'rowing' movement. Keep the weights touching and close to your body, so your elbows point outwards in a 'V' shape. Hold at the top and then slowly descend to the starting position.

Weights to chin

Core engaged

1 Stand with your feet shoulder-width apart, knees slightly bent and spine neutral. Hold a weight in each hand, with your elbows slightly bent, palms facing forwards and the ends of the weights just touching in front of you.

Rear delt fly

This drill tightens the backs of the shoulders. If you have a tendency to slouch, it will help you to improve your posture and make you stand up straight.

Bend at hips

Elbow slightly bent

1 Stand with both feet on the floor, shoulder-width apart, and bend forwards at the hips, so that your back is at a right angle to your legs. Hold a weight in your left hand, palm facing inwards, and let your right arm hang down. Both elbows and knees should be very slightly bent.

2 Bring your left arm out to the side until the weight reaches shoulder height, keeping your elbow slightly bent. Bring it back down to the starting point then repeat on the opposite side.

Feet hip-width apart

Standing scarecrow

This is a great one for working your rotator cuff – the group of muscles and tendons that stabilize your shoulder joint.

1 Stand with your feet shoulder-width apart and a weight in each hand. Extend your arms out to the sides in line with your shoulders then bend your elbows so that your forearms are pointing down and your palms are facing backwards.

Elbows at right angles

2 Keeping your upper arms level with your shoulders, rotate and lift the weights up so that your forearms point up and your palms face forwards. Rotate back down again, and repeat.

Feet hip-width apart

TOP TIP

Hit the wall? Take a deep breath and then scale it.

Dumbbell hammer

You'll work your biceps hard with this hammer curl. Roll your shoulders backwards before you start to get the correct posture and keep your core braced throughout.

1 With your feet shoulder-width apart, knees soft, shoulders back and core braced, hold your dumbbells by your sides, palms facing inwards.

Shoulders back

Squeeze weights

Core engaged

2 Curl your arms upwards, bending at the elbow, until the weights reach the tops of your shoulders. Keep your arms close to your sides, then squeeze your weights tightly to create some tension. When you reach the top, pause, lower the weights and repeat.

TOP TIP

Every muscle you develop burns more fat, so push yourself thin.

Dumbbell bicep curl

This drill works a different part of the biceps from the Dumbbell Hammer, as you bring your weights out wider on the lift. Be sure to avoid tensing your neck.

Weights to shoulder height

1 With your feet shoulder-width apart, knees soft, shoulders back and core braced, hold the dumbbells by your sides, palms facing inwards.

2 Bend your elbows and raise the weights to shoulder height, rotating your wrists as you do so. This time bring them outwards so that they finish outside the edges of your shoulders. Hold at the top, then lower your weights and repeat.

Running biceps

Get a little bounce in this drill, as if you are actually running, to build tone in your biceps and forearms. It's performed at speed, so you'll be getting some cardio, too.

1 Stand with feet shoulder-width apart, back straight and knees slightly bent. Hold one weight in your right hand at chest height, the other down by your hip, both palms facing inwards.

2 Simultaneously bring your left weight up to chest height and let your right weight drop down without locking your elbow. Get a rapid running movement going – one side up and the other down – until you feel a bit puffed out.

Concentration curl

Performed properly, this exercise will give you the ultimate in toned biceps.
Concentrate on a smooth up–down movement and keep your wrists straight.

1 Sit on a chair or bench with your knees bent and your feet flat on the floor and spread wide apart. Lean forwards slightly, keeping your eyes on the horizon. Hold a weight in your right hand, palm facing inwards, and let it drop straight down. Brace your right elbow on the inside of your thigh.

2 Curl the weight up then down again in a continuous movement, without locking your elbow. Complete the repetitions then switch the weight to your left hand and repeat.

Dumbbell overhead press

This drill will work your triceps. Placing your non-working hand on your abdomen will remind you to keep your core braced, which will help you to avoid neck strain.

Arm straight

Chin up

Hand on abs

1 Stand with your feet shoulder-width apart, left hand on your abdominals and right hand holding a weight straight up in the air, palm facing forwards. Keep your eyes on the horizon.

2 Slowly bend your right elbow to 90 degrees, without moving your upper arm, so that the weight drops behind your head. Lower the weight as far as you can. Stop, then contract your triceps to drive it back up again. Change arms and repeat.

TOP TIP

Got a goal you really want to achieve? Then up the ante and put your whole mind into the drill.

Dumbbell kickback

To get a good contraction of your triceps during this drill, make sure that the only movement is in your elbow joint and that you are not swinging from the shoulder.

1 Stand with your left foot forwards and your right foot back, the front knee slightly bent to give you a lower centre of gravity. Rest your left hand on your thigh and hold a weight in your right hand. Bow forwards, and bend your right arm to bring your weight up to waist level.

90-degree angle (elbow)

Weight at waist height

Front knee slightly bent

2 Keeping your right shoulder and elbow in a line, straighten your elbow until your arm is stretching behind you and the triceps muscle is fully contracted. Bend your elbow to return the weight to the starting position. Repeat with the weight in your other hand.

Chair dip

This drill works on strengthening, conditioning and toning your triceps and shoulder muscles. Beginners can do it with their legs bent and feet flat on the floor.

Look straight ahead

2 Lower yourself down until your elbows are bent at right angles, keeping your back straight. Push yourself back up again, until your arms are straight once more.

Legs straight

1 Sit on a chair or bench with your hands on the edge alongside your butt. Curl your fingers over the edge, support your bodyweight with your arms and lift yourself up off of the chair or bench.

Skull crusher

This is a slow, controlled movement that works your triceps hard. Keep a firm grip on your weights so you don't take the name of the exercise too literally!

1 Lie on the floor with your knees bent and feet flat. Hold your weights straight up above your shoulders, palms facing inwards. Keep your chin up.

2 Bend your elbows so that the weights come back and skim the sides of your head. Use your elbows like a hinge, keeping your upper arms in the same position, and bringing the weights down and then straight back up again.

Knees bent

Elbows like hinges

Feet flat

MULTIJOINT EXERCISES COMBINE different movements into a flowing sequence to work a broader range of muscles in one go. Are they easy? No. But work hard at them and you'll get results – fast.

Squat thrust

Squat thrusts are much more dynamic than a normal shoulder press or squat because they really work your abs, arms and legs.

1 Stand with your feet shoulder-width apart, back straight and core braced. With your eyes on the horizon, hold a weight in both hands, just below your chin, palms facing inwards.

2 Drop down into a squat, drive your hips back and stick out your butt. Keep your elbows relaxed and your head up, and keep looking straight ahead.

3 Drive the dumbbell straight up over your head in an explosive movement, straightening your legs and body at the same time. Use your core muscles to provide power. Hold at the top then return to your starting point.

Deadlift row

This drill combines the Deadlift (see page 108) and the Dumbbell Row (see page 129) for maximum impact. Get moving and you'll work your whole body at once.

1 Stand with your legs a little wider than shoulder-width apart. Hold a weight in your right hand, palm facing inwards. Bow forwards into deadlift position, driving your butt out.

2 Perform a row, bending your right elbow to bring the weight up to waist level.

3 Squeeze your glutes and drive up to standing position, maintaining a neutral spine. Do your first set of repetitions then change arms to work the other side.

spine neutral

Press-up plank

This is a tough, nasty drill that combines the press-up and the plank. It's seriously challenging but fantastic for building upper body strength, so persevere.

1 Start in press-up position with your hands palms down on the floor beneath your shoulders, arms straight and toes tucked under. Brace your core and keep your back and legs straight and strong.

2 Bend your elbows to lower your body halfway down, keeping your eyes on the floor. Stop and hold when you have a 90-degree bend at the elbows.

3 Lower yourself again, this time down to just above the ground. Pause then drive yourself straight up to the top of the press-up plank again.

Legs straight

Core braced

Toes tucked under

Hands under shoulders

Bicep curl, press extension

This drill is a series of three movements that will give your triceps and biceps a good workout. Keep your core stable so you don't lose your balance.

1 Stand with your feet shoulder-width apart and shoulders back. Hold the weights by your side, palms facing inwards and your elbows slightly bent.

2 Curl up your arms, raising the weights to just above shoulder height, letting your elbows pull slightly away from your body. Hold for a few seconds.

3 Press up your weights, using your core for stability, until your arms are stretched above your head, the weights directly over your shoulders. Hold for a few seconds.

4 Bend your elbows so that the weights drop behind your head, and bring your hands together so that they are almost touching. Keep your shoulders back. Hold for a few seconds, then reverse the whole movement back to the starting position.

Clean

In this combination of a squat and a Deadlift (see page 108), you'll use your glutes, hips and abs to provide the explosive power to drive you upwards into a jump.

Weight up to shoulder

Arm out for balance

2 Simultaneously curl the weight up to shoulder height and jump into the air. Land softly and drop straight back down into the starting position. Repeat.

Legs just wider than shoulders

1 Stand with your legs a little wider than shoulder-width apart and a neutral spine, then bow forwards into the deadlift position, driving your butt out. Hold a weight in your right hand, palm facing inwards, and raise your left arm out to the side for balance.

Woodchopper

This drill works your upper body as you rotate, and tones and conditions your thighs and lower body through the swing and squat. The movement is like chopping wood.

1 Stand with your feet a little wider than shoulder-width apart and your legs straight. Hold a dumbbell with both hands, palms facing inwards, and lift it up beyond your right shoulder, with your arms outstretched.

2 Swing the dumbbell down in front of you to chest height, arms still outstretched as if you are about to bring it down on a pile of wood. At the same time, lower your body into a semi-squat.

3 Swing the dumbbell down past your left thigh, twisting your abdomen as you go. You should feel a stretch on your right-hand side. Keep your arms outstretched, and hold the squat position for a few seconds. Reverse up to the starting position and repeat in a smooth, flowing movement, then switch directions and start with the weight beyond your left shoulder.

Feel the stretch in your side

TOP TIP

Get mad about the way you're looking, and let your body know you mean business.

Zombie

The Zombie isn't for beginners, but it's worth mastering for the whole-body strength and cardio workout it gives. It helps you develop great balance and burn calories.

1 Stand with your feet hip-width apart, knees bent, butt out and arms stretched behind you, palms facing inwards. Keep your eyes on the horizon.

2 Swing your arms forwards, and JUMP! Push up out of your legs and hips to get some height, swinging your hands up to face level.

3 Bend your knees as you land and bring your elbows to your sides. Keep looking forwards and push your butt right out.

4 Lower yourself until you're sitting on the floor, with knees bent and feet flat. Rest your hands on the floor by your hips.

5 Use your abdominal muscles to lower your upper body to the floor, keeping your knees bent. Slide your arms forwards on the floor at either side of your body.

6 Straighten your legs and clasp your hands into a prayer position in front of your chest, fingertips pointing upwards. Then it's back up into the starting position to do some more!

Commando

**This is serious American military stuff, working those abs, delts and pecs.
Get down and dirty and you could become the next Action Man – or GI Jane.**

1 Get yourself into a plank position (see page 133),
body straight, facing down, arms bent at right angles,
bodyweight resting on your forearms and toes.

2 Shift your weight on to your left forearm and push up
on to your right hand, keeping your body and legs in
a straight line.

3 Push up on your left hand until both your arms are fully
extended, but don't lock your elbows. Hold the position
for a few seconds.

4 Come back down on to your right elbow, and then your
left, until you reach the starting position again.

Prone abductor

This is a great exercise for working your hip abductors and abdominals. Get your legs well off the ground to make sure you give those abs a good workout.

Core engaged

1 Lie flat on your back, arms resting on the floor beside you, palms down, and your chin up. Bracing your core, raise your feet off the floor as high as you can, keeping your legs together.

2 Open your legs into a 'V' shape – as wide as you can – and bring them back in again. This is a quick in–out movement, like scissors. Lower to the floor and repeat.

Legs wide apart

Palms facing down

Lower back on floor

Cool-down exercises

AFTER ANY EXERCISE, you should spend 5–10 minutes cooling down and getting your body back to normal. You need to reduce your heart rate, disperse excess adrenaline and loosen up tight muscles so that they don't cramp or tear.

Side stretch

Stand with your feet flat on the floor, slightly wider than shoulder-width apart, knees slightly bent. Hold your left arm across your abs and bring your right arm straight up into the air, palm facing forwards. Stretch over to your left as far as you can and hold for 10–15 seconds. Change arms and repeat.

Shoulder stretch

Stand with your feet shoulder-width apart, knees bent and butt sticking out. Clasp your hands in front of you, palms facing outwards, and push into them, feeling the stretch between your shoulder blades. Hold for 10–15 seconds.

Balistic stretch, arms crossed

Stand with your feet shoulder-width apart and your knees slightly bent. Stretch your arms across your chest in opposite directions, right arm to the left and left arm to the right. Have your right arm above your left for the first stretch, then swap for the repetition. Stretch out and hold for 10–15 seconds each time.

Chest stretch

Stand with your feet shoulder-width apart and your hands resting on your lower back. Keeping your head up and your shoulders down, squeeze your elbows together and feel your chest opening. Hold for 10–15 seconds, release and repeat.

Tricep stretch

Stand with your feet hip-width apart and stretch your right arm across your chest so the hand extends past your left shoulder. Bend your left arm upwards, palm facing you, and press against your right elbow until you feel a stretch in your triceps. Hold for 10–15 seconds then repeat with the opposite arms.

Hamstring stretch

There are lots of ways to do hamstring stretches, but this one can be done any time, anywhere, whether in a gym, your sitting room or after a run.

From standing position, step your left leg forwards and rest on your heel. Bend your right knee and place your hands on it, keeping your upper body straight and sitting your weight back into your butt. Point your left toe upwards and keep your heel on the floor, and you'll feel a stretch at the back of your left leg. Hold for 15–20 seconds, then change legs.

Hips back

Right knee bent

TOP TIP

Stretch until you feel the burn. Tight hamstrings can cause injury.

Pull toe back

Heel on floor

Quad stretch

This loosens up the fronts of your thighs (quads). Lean on a chair or the wall for support if you can't keep your balance.

Calf stretch

Calves can get tight after running or jumping, so always stretch out after an exercise session involving either.

Stand with feet together, body straight, knees aligned and shoulders back. Rest your weight on your left leg and bend your right leg up behind you, reaching behind with your right hand to grab the front of your foot. Pull your foot up as far as you can. Bow forwards for an even better stretch. Hold for 20 seconds, then swap legs and repeat.

Take a big stride forwards with your left leg. Bend your left knee, while pushing your right heel down into the floor. You'll feel the stretch in your right calf. Hold for 20 seconds, then switch legs and repeat.

Your six-week fitness plan

Now it's time to put all the exercises and cardio work together into your exercise plan. The programme is six weeks long, with something to do almost every day of the week. Follow it exactly and you'll lose weight. Add another cardio session and you'll lose more. The idea is to start with five workouts per week, and by the end of six weeks, you'll be up to ten.

The basics
Choose the cardio you want and then fit in the workouts we've chosen for you, as listed on pages 182–183. The number of reps of each exercise will depend on your fitness level and so will the minutes of rest you're allowed. Put yourself in one of the fitness levels below. Be honest – there's no point in pushing yourself beyond your capabilities and you'll soon be moving on to the next level.

Beginner Most Biggest Losers start off as exercise beginners. If you don't normally do anything more strenuous than walk around the supermarket, this is your category. Start by doing 15 reps of each exercise and resting for a maximum of 45 seconds between exercises, but increase the reps and decrease the rest as soon as you feel able. Start by completing one whole set, but if you finish in under an hour, go back to the beginning and start again.

Intermediate Do you think of yourself as reasonably fit? If you can breathe easily after running up the stairs, start here by doing 20 reps of each exercise, with a rest between each of a maximum of 30 seconds. You should manage 2–3 sets per session.

Advanced You've got to be pretty fit to reach this point. You'll know when you are here because you can confidently complete 25 reps of each exercise with a rest of only 15 seconds between each, and you could be managing as many as 5 sets at a time.

Circuits
The Hi-intensity Tone and Xpress Workouts (see pages 180 and 181) are designed as circuits. This means going through the set as fast as you can, completing each exercise only once and resting for no more than 5 seconds in between. When you get to the end, go straight back to the beginning and continue until your hour is up! These workouts are convenient if you only have 20 minutes or half an hour to spare, but be sure to do more later in the day so you've managed an hour in total.

Warming and cooling
Always take 10 minutes to warm up before you exercise and another 5 minutes to cool down afterwards, working through the exercises on pages 100–103 for the warm-up and pages 170–173 for the cool-down. This is an essential part of the programme, to prevent injuries and protect your muscles and joints. Afterwards you'll be feeling energized and ready to tackle tomorrow's challenge.

YOUR FITNESS PROGRAMME

	REPS	SETS	REST BETWEEN EXERCISES
Beginner	**15**	**1**	**45 seconds max**
Intermediate	**20**	**2–3**	**30 seconds max**
Advanced	**25**	**3–5**	**15 seconds max**

YOUR FITNESS PROGRAMME

Total body blast
A full-body workout to wake you up in the morning and get your muscles tingling.

Dumbbell fly
(see page 122)

One-armed row
(see page 131)

Static lunge
(see page 110)

Sideways step-up
(see page 117)

Dumbbell bicep curl
(see page 153)

Chair dip
(see page 158)

Plank
(see page 133)

Superman crunch
(see page 137)

Woodchopper
(see page 165)

Squat thrust
(see page 160)

Armageddon
Believe me – you'll feel the effects of this one from top to toe.

Bodyweight press-up (see page 119)

Dumbbell row
(see page 129)

Single-leg plyometric hop
(see page 116)

Frog squat
(see page 115)

21 bicep curls
(see page 143)

Dumbbell kickback
(see page 157)

Plank
(see page 133)

Superman crunch
(see page 137)

Woodchopper
(see page 165)

Squat thrust
(see page 160)

Body fat burner
There are cardio elements in here, as well as muscle-building moves.

Plyometric push-up
(see page 124)

Commando
(see page 168)

Dumbbell row
(see page 129)

Dumbbell squat
(see page 106)

Clean
(see page 164)

Chair dip
(see page 158)

Concentration curl
(see page 155)

Standing scarecrow
(see page 151)

Plank
(see page 133)

Superman crunch
(see page 137)

Totally toned
Toning, firming and strengthening moves for all your wobbly bits.

Dumbbell chest press
(see page 126)

Dumbbell
overhead press
(see page 156)

Anterior
shoulder raise
(see page 147)

Bicep curl,
press extension
(see page 163)

Skull crusher
(see page 159)

Prone abductor
(see page 169)

Twisting windmill
(see page 141)

Dumbbell
side bend
(see page 139)

Woodchopper
(see page 165)

Squat thrust
(see page 160)

Up front & personal
This workout concentrates on the pecs, for all you guys with 'moobs'.

Rotational push-up
(see page 120)

Dumbbell close-grip chest press
(see page 127)

Dumbbell fly single arm
(see page 123)

One-armed row
(see page 131)

Moving lunge
(see page 111)

Running biceps
(see page 154)

Chair dip
(see page 158)

Commando
(see page 168)

Reverse crunch
(see page 136)

Triple crunch
(see page 135)

Back to front
Strengthening your back with this workout will help to prevent injury.

Lower back raise
(see page 130)

Dumbbell row
(see page 129)

Prone abductor
(see pages 169)

Woodchopper
(see page 165)

Single-leg deadlift
(see page 109)

Press-up plank
(see page 162)

Skull crusher
(see page 159)

One-armed row
(see page 131)

Bicep curl, press extension
(see page 163)

Dumbbell side bend
(see page 139)

Lovely legs   Trim your pins with this strengthening workout.

Deadlift
(see page 108)

Prone abductor
(see page 169)

Sideways step-up
(see page 117)

**Bulgarian
split squat**
(see page 112)

Frog squat
(see page 115)

Isometric squat
(see page 113)

Abdominal twist
(see page 140)

Plank
(see page 133)

**Dumbbell
side bend**
(see page 139)

Reverse crunch
(see page 136)

Awesome arms   Define your triceps, biceps and delts so you look great in short sleeves.

Dumbbell chest press
(see page 126)

Dumbbell kickback
(see page 157)

Concentration curl
(see page 155)

Skull crusher
(see page 159)

Running biceps
(see page 154)

**Dumbbell double
standing press**
(see page 145)

Dumbbell row
(see page 129)

Standing scarecrow
(see page 151)

Rear delt fly
(see page 150)

Diamond push-up
(see page 125)

YOUR FITNESS PROGRAMME

Hi-intensity tone
Work through these exercises at speed, doing just one of each before going on to the next. When you get to the end, start again!

Zombie
(see pages 166–167)

Commando
(see page 168)

Sideways step-up
(see page 117)

One-armed row
(see page 131)

Dumbbell chest press
(see page 126)

Lower back raise
(see page 130)

Woodchopper
(see page 165)

Dumbbell single standing press
(see page 144)

Bicep curl, press extension
(see page 163)

Reverse crunch
(see page 136)

Strictly stomach
Everyone wants a flat stomach and these ab-tightening exercises will get you well on the way to achieving just that.

Squat thrust
(see page 160)

Woodchopper
(see page 165)

Triple crunch
(see page 135)

Commando
(see page 168)

Superman crunch
(see page 137)

Plank
(see page 133)

Dumbbell Russian twist
(see page 138)

Lower back raise
(see page 130)

Zombie (see pages 166–167)

Dumbbell crunch
(see page 134)

The xpress workout

Do one of each with a maximum of 5 seconds' rest in between and you should be able to complete this workout in 20–30 minutes.

Plyometric dumbbell chest press into crunch (see page 121)

Rear delt fly (see page 150)

Bulgarian split squat (see page 112)

Dumbbell squat kick (see page 114)

Running biceps (see page 154)

Chair dip (see page 158)

Single-leg plyometric hop (see page 116)

Plank (see page 133)

Superman crunch (see page 137)

Moving lunge (see page 111)

20-minute mash-up

Do this instead of a longer workout when you are running short of time. Just do one repetition of each.

Rotational push-up (see page 120)

One-armed row (see page 131)

Squat thrust (see page 160)

Dumbbell push press (see page 148)

Plyometric squat (see page 107)

Sideways step-up (see page 117)

Abdominal twist (see page 140)

Dumbbell Russian twist (see page 138)

Chair dip (see page 158)

Dumbbell hammer (see page 152)

Weekly workout guide

Follow this guide, choosing any cardio activity you like and sustaining it for 60 minutes – or two sessions of 30 minutes or three of 20. Mix and match the sets of exercises but make sure you do them all and don't just stick to your favourites. You can change the rest days to fit in with your schedule.

Week one	
Monday	Cardio
Tuesday	Total body blast (see page 176)
Wednesday	Cardio
Thursday	Rest
Friday	Totally toned (see page 177)
Saturday	Cardio
Sunday	Rest
Week two	
Monday	Cardio
Tuesday	20-minute mash-up x 3 (see page 181)
Wednesday	Cardio
Thursday	Rest
Friday	Hi-intensity tone (see page 180)
Saturday	Cardio
Sunday	Rest
Week three	
Monday	Cardio / Strictly stomach (see page 180)
Tuesday	Armageddon (see page 176)
Wednesday	Cardio / Body fat burner (see page 177)
Thursday	Rest
Friday	Back to front (see page 178)
Saturday	Cardio
Sunday	Rest

Week four	
Monday	Cardio / Up front & personal (see page 178)
Tuesday	Lovely legs (see page 179)
Wednesday	Cardio / The xpress workout (see page 181)
Thursday	Rest
Friday	Cardio / Total body blast (see page 176)
Saturday	Hi-intensity tone (see page 180)
Sunday	Rest
Week five	
Monday	Cardio / 20-minute mash-up (see page 181)
Tuesday	Back to front (see page 178)
Wednesday	Cardio
Thursday	Rest
Friday	Cardio / Armageddon (see page 176)
Saturday	Strictly stomach (see page 180)
Sunday	Cardio
Week six	
Monday	Totally toned (see page 177)
Tuesday	Cardio / The xpress workout (see page 181)
Wednesday	Body fat burner (see page 177)
Thursday	Cardio / Lovely legs (see page 179)
Friday	Total body blast (see page 176)
Saturday	Cardio / Back to front (see page 178)
Sunday	Hi-intensity tone (see page 180)

Maintaining your ideal weight

Congratulations! If you've made it through the six-week programme you are officially a Biggest Loser. You may have finished one journey, but you are now at the beginning of another – a new way of living that will keep off the kilos and ensure health and wellbeing for years to come.

Slim for life

If you haven't been cheating, you'll already have lost a big chunk of weight, but you may not have reached your final target yet.

Set a new goal for another six weeks and continue to follow the programme, making time for at least ten exercise sessions a week. It may take many more months of hard work, but you can and will succeed.

Once you reach your final target, it's not an excuse to go back to gorging on takeaways in front of the telly while your dumbbells gather dust in the corner. The Biggest Loser healthy eating plan is a programme for life. When you reach your target weight, you increase the number of portions you eat of each food group until you find a level that keeps your weight steady. The secret is to continue to eat the same balance of foods, focusing on plenty of fresh fruit and vegetables, lean proteins, healthy wholegrain carbohydrates and the minimum of fat. Your plate should look the same as it did when you were in the losing phase; you can simply eat a little more.

The people who lose weight and keep it off long-term are the ones who make exercise a feature of their daily life. By building muscle instead of fat stores, you'll keep your metabolic rate high and you'll continue to look and feel great. Stop exercising and the kilos will slip back on. Simple as that.

Stay looking good
To keep looking good you need to keep an eye on the ball. Weigh yourself once a week, be aware of the fit of your clothes and keep up your food diary so that you don't slip back into old habits. Plan your meals in advance so you don't succumb to temptation while hungry, and keep your 'before' picture in view to remind you of how much you have achieved already and provide the inspiration to carry on.

Dealing with setbacks

There will be times when you are tempted to revert to your old habits and lose your motivation to remain trim, fit and healthy. The secret is never to give up.

Remind yourself of the amazing feat you've already achieved and keep that 'before' picture somewhere that you can look at it regularly. Focus on how much better you feel – physically and emotionally – and how your self-confidence and self-esteem has soared.

Stay positive. Don't let moments of low self-esteem drag you down. Strive hard for something that is important to you and don't be afraid to win.

Continue to give yourself that weekly weigh-in, first thing in the morning, to ensure the kilos aren't creeping back on. Are your clothes fitting nicely? No waistbands starting to dig in or buttons that won't fasten? Can you pinch more than an inch anywhere? If your weight is increasing, get straight back on the programme and burn off the excess. You'll be amazed how quickly you'll manage this now that your body is working more efficiently.

If you fall off the wagon, the trick is to jump right back on. Don't look at it as permission to go back down your old, unhealthy path. Buy a new exercise DVD and challenge yourself to complete all the moves. Start keeping your Biggest Loser notebook again, jotting down everything you eat and the way

you felt at the time. Were you bored, tired or upset about something when you ate that jam doughnut? Recognizing when problems are likely to occur is the first step to avoiding them. Be diligent about doing some extra cardio to make up for any binges and your weight will stay under control.

Tips to keep you on track
Here are a few quick fixes if you lose focus:
- Don't look at exercise as a chore; make it part of your daily routine, like brushing your teeth. You've trained your body to want to exercise, and as long as you keep up the momentum, you'll find it easy to continue.
- Find a workout partner. Not only will this inspire a little healthy competition, but you'll find the experience of exercising more fun if it's social.
- Learn to say 'no'. You don't want the extra drinks at happy hour or the all-you-can-eat Chinese because they aren't going to help you to stick at your target weight and stay healthy.
- Don't worry about yesterday or tomorrow. Do your best today.

Positive reinforcement
Take pride in your successes and celebrate your massive victory. Weight loss is not easy, but you did it. Develop a series of positive affirmations to reinforce your self-belief: 'I am a Biggest Loser'; 'I can achieve anything I set my mind to'; 'I am slim, healthy and strong and I love my new life'. You get the picture.

MAINTAINING YOUR IDEAL WEIGHT

A whole new you

Celebrate your new size by having some 'after' pictures taken that you can compare with the 'before' ones to see how far you've come. It's a great excuse for a makeover and maybe you'll even feel good enough to pose for a bikini shot. Good for you!

You've got all the tools you need to stay in this shape for life, but don't let yourself get complacent. Always remember how you felt when you were fat and focus on the differences in your life now.

Choose your friends wisely

There may be some friends who liked you better when you were fat; perhaps they feel threatened by your success or envious of your new look. These are not the people who will help you stay committed to your new healthy lifestyle. Spend less time with them and create a new circle of friends who enjoy being active in their leisure hours, and will join you for cycling trips or a game of tennis. Surround yourself with people who love what you've achieved and who will actively encourage you to continue to succeed.

Keep things varied

Although it can be tempting to stick with what you know, exercising and eating the same way day after day in order to maintain your weight can get boring. Put the spice back into your life. Try out some exciting new low-fat recipes and experiment with different foods and styles of cooking. Join a dance class; treat yourself to membership at a gym where you can try new classes and equipment; or book a holiday where you can try waterskiing or white-water rafting for a real change.

Go shopping

Buy some new clothes that reflect your new-found self-confidence. If you've been hiding your overweight body under swathes of oversized clothing for years, you may find it difficult to accept that your wardrobe can be transformed by the options now open to someone of your size and shape. Yes, you can wear slinky evening dresses or pencil skirts with a tucked-in blouse. Guys, you can dig out your old jeans and t-shirts and get a slim new suit. Try it and see. Keep yourself looking good with a new haircut or indulge in a beauty treatment once in a while to pamper yourself. You are worth it.

Believe in yourself

We are here to tell you that anything and everything is possible if you believe in yourself. You'll find the time to exercise; you'll look in the mirror and know that things have changed. You'll see that you are walking taller; you'll realize that you can take slip-ups in your stride and just carry on. You will learn that one mistake does not mean the end of your healthy lifestyle. You can shrug it off and move on.

You've created new habits – and a new you. You eat well, you exercise, you look great. And, you know what? You know that, too.

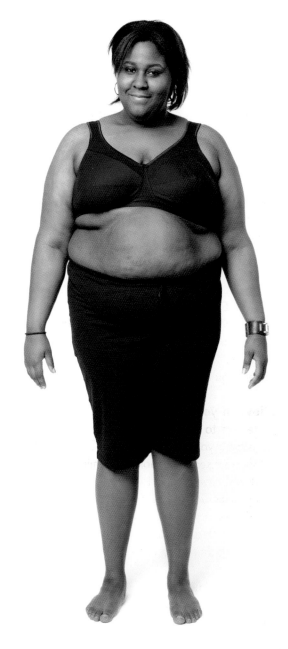

Before

After

Sadie

Index

The Biggest Loser Meal Replacement Programme is a weight loss system designed to provide effective and sustainable results. The programme involves replacing two meals each day with delicious shakes, soups and bars and eating a range of healthy foods in between as well as a balanced evening meal.

The Biggest Loser Meal Replacement products are portion-controlled, nutritionally-balanced 'meals' that contain all of the energy, protein, fibre, vitamins and minerals you need to lose weight in a healthy and sustainable way. The Programme also helps you to set healthy habits to ensure your weight loss results are maintained over a long period of time. They can also help to break bad lifestyle habits, such as skipping breakfast, which can lead to weight gain.

Meal Replacement programmes have increasing support amongst the scientific and healthcare community with a wide range of international studies backing their effectiveness. They can provide great short-term results to keep you motivated to continue your weight-loss journey as well as setting you up to maintain those results over a longer period of time.

For weight loss that's easy, convenient and affordable, join The Biggest Loser Club today. This all new website has helped The Biggest Loser contestants to achieve amazing results, and now it's here for you, too.

For as little as £2.50 a week, you'll get a personalized weight-loss programme including delicious meals, easy-to-follow exercise plans and inspiring video messages from trainers Richard and Angie.

Plus, you'll experience all the great features used by the contestants including the **online diary**, a **nutrition library** of over **20,000 foods,** a **buzzing community** and **step-by-step instructions and videos** for more than **500 exercises.**

It's simple to use and easy to stick to, so start your transformation today at
www.biggestloserclub.co.uk